PARTICIPANT

THE **5** W'S

WHO * WHAT * WHERE * WHEN * WHY

# of Our Catholic Faith
AND HOW WE LIVE IT

PARTICIPANT

THE 5 W'S

WHO * WHAT * WHERE * WHEN * WHY

of Our Catholic Faith
AND HOW WE LIVE IT

Edited by Mary Carol Kendzia

Liguori
LIGUORI, MISSOURI

Imprimi Potest: Harry Grile, CSsR
Provincial, Denver Province, The Redemptorists

Imprimatur: "In accordance with c. 823-830, permission to publish has been granted on January 4, 2011, by the Most Reverend Thomas J. Tobin, Bishop, Diocese of Providence, Rhode Island. Permission to publish is an indication that nothing contrary to Church teaching is contained in this work. It does not imply any endorsement of the opinions expressed in the publication; nor is any liability assumed by this permission."

Published by Liguori Publications
Liguori, Missouri 63057
To order, call 800-325-9521, or visit www.liguori.org.

Library of Congress Cataloging-in-Publication Data

The 5 W's of our Catholic faith : who, what, where, when, why...and how we live it: participant / edited by Mary Carol Kendzia.—1st ed.
     p. cm.
 ISBN 978-0-7648-1987-2
 1. Catholic Church—Doctrines. 2. Theology, Doctrinal—Popular works. I. Kendzia, Mary Carol. II. Title: Five W's of our Catholic faith.
 BX1754.A15 2010
 230'.2—dc22
 2010040789

Liguori Publications, a nonprofit corporation, is an apostolate of the Redemptorists. To learn more about the Redemptorists, visit Redemptorists.com.

Printed in the United States of America
15 14 13 12 11   5 4 3 2 1
First edition

Contents

Introduction

Who are you, and what is it that you want to know about the Catholic Church?

- Are you a cradle Catholic—now in your forties, fifties, or sixties—wondering, where do I fit in with the Catholic Church at this point in my life? Why are so many things different from what I grew up with? How can I grow in my faith and in my spiritual practice?

- Or are you a young adult, developing a career or starting a family, hoping to find a renewed sense of place within the Church that will provide guidance and companionship for this part of your life journey?

- Perhaps you are a non-Catholic who is curious about the Catholic faith: Is entrance into the Church a path you may want to pursue?

- You might be a teen in the exciting and challenging time of preparation for the sacrament of confirmation, or a college student looking to connect on a deeper level with the basics of Catholicism.

- Maybe you are in the latter part of life, inquisitive and looking to see the Church with new eyes, sharing questions, insights, and experiences with other Catholics.

No matter who you are or where in your faith journey you may be at this moment, this book has much to offer you. Composed of simple, brief overviews, it looks at the basic tenets of the Catholic faith—the Church, your faith journey, Scripture, Jesus Christ, sacraments, Christian living, and prayer—presenting highlights and key points in each of these areas.

You'll discover who built up the Church, from the early Christian communities through today, and what it is that makes the Church unique among Christian denominations. When did key moments occur in the Church, and where did its growth take place? Why do we gather for Mass on Sunday, and how do traditional practices such as saying the rosary and perpetual adoration fit in with the modern Church?

Perhaps most important is the "how" of this book: How do I fit in with the people of God? How does Jesus' directive to "Go, make disciples of all" fit into my life? How do I read and understand Scripture in a way that can enrich my faith? How do my everyday choices reflect my Catholic faith? How do I practice contemplative prayer?

Each session in this ten-part study brings participants to a deeper level of knowledge and understanding about the Catholic faith. The approach used in this series touches on critical themes and topics in a simple yet engaging manner, and offers questions for further reflection and/or discussion.

Ideally, this resource should be used within a group, whether based in the parish, at a retreat center, or in a home as part of a small Christian community. This type of setting provides a forum for interaction among participants, with the opportunity for sharing questions, insights, and experiences with each other.

This book can also be used by individuals. In this case, it would be good to keep a journal to record thoughts and reflections on the questions that follow each section. These can be shared with a priest, friend, or spiritual director if so desired.

Whoever you are and in whatever way you use this book to take a deeper journey into the Catholic faith, you take with you the wisdom of many fellow travelers with years of experience and insight. The Catholic faith is a multi-faceted jewel. May it illuminate your heart, mind, and soul as you discover the richness it has to offer.

We Are the Church

WHO is the Church?

WHAT was religion to the early Christians?

WHERE did the ethics and morals of Christianity originate?

WHEN did the Eastern church separate from Rome?

WHY does the Church continue to be a sign of Christ's presence in the world?

Opening Song: "Sing a New Church," by Dolores Dufner, OSB, or a hymn of your choice

Opening Prayer: God of all creation, you have called us to this community known as the Catholic Church. Bless our work during this session today, that we may come to better understand who we are and where we come from as members of this Church. Open our minds and our hearts to your word, and to the words of those gathered here with us today. Inspire us with your spirit, and guide us in the way of Jesus, the Christ. Amen.

Reading: Acts 2:42–47

Spend a moment in quiet reflection.

Founded by Christ

The word "Church" has many different meanings. For Catholics, however, Church is more than a building, or a group of people, or a liturgy. The truth is expressed at the beginning of Mass: "The grace of our Lord Jesus Christ and the love of God and the fellowship of the Holy Spirit be with you all."

It is here that our unity as Christians lies. For the Church is people: people united, not by something, not a building, or a hierarchy, or a group, but by someone.

The Second Vatican Council points out that the Church shines forth as "a people made one with the unity of the Father, the Son, and the Holy Spirit" (Dogmatic Constitution on the Church, # 4). The Church is the community of all those who have been drawn into the life of God. The Church is the continuing presence of Christ leading people to the vision of God. The Church is a people with one "soul"—the Holy Spirit dwelling in their hearts.

We are made in the image and likeness of God, and since God is "community" (Father, Son, and Holy Spirit), we need community.

Because the Church is made up of human beings who are not perfect, it is to be expected that the Church will be less than perfect. Jesus knew that those who would represent him were subject to failure. Peter denied him three times, but Jesus, after his resurrection, gave Peter a threefold commission to care for his flock (John 21:15–18). The apostles ran away when Jesus was arrested, and yet he appeared to them after his resurrection and sent them to preach the Gospel to all nations (Matthew 28:16–20).

The early Church had all the problems found in churches today. There were liars and hypocrites (Acts 5:1–11). There were complaints of unfairness (Acts 6:1). There were those who used religion for personal gain (Acts 8:9–24). There were disagreements about doctrine (Acts 15). There were conflicts among Church leaders (Acts 15:36–41). There were sermons that failed to make an impact upon the preacher's audience (Acts 17:22–34), and sermons so long that they put people to sleep (Acts 20:7–12). There were questions about pastors' salaries, disorder at worship ceremonies, scandal, and neglect of the poor (1 Corinthians 5–11). There were all the problems that arise when people try to follow Jesus and fall short of the mark because of human weakness and sin.

> *"You are the body of Christ."*
> 1 CORINTHIANS 12:27

Of course, there were also heroes (Acts 7), holiness (Acts 2:42–47), and generosity (Acts 4:32–37). If there were laws and leaders, it was because no society can exist without them (Acts 6:1–7). If there were rituals, it was because these were faithful responses to Christ's will (1 Corinthians 11:23–26). If there were times when the followers of Jesus failed him, there were also times when they were heroic in professing his Gospel (Acts 4:1–22).

Jesus came to draw us into the "community love" of the Trinity. He lived, died, and rose to bring all people into one family (John 10:16–18). At the Last Supper, he asked us to love one another as he loves us (John 15:12). He prayed that we would be one, as he and the Father are one (John 17:20–21). He formed the community of believers into the sign of his continuing presence on earth. He said, "For where two or three are gathered in my name, I am there among them" (Matthew 18:20).

HOW We Live It

- *What are some of the communities that influence and nourish your life, for example, family, friends, co-workers, neighborhood, parish, or civic groups?*

- *How do you feel about the fact that the Church is an imperfect body of people?*

From the Beginning

The descent of the Holy Spirit on Pentecost is celebrated as the "Birthday of the Church."

After Jesus ascended, the disciples went to the upper room and prayed. They must have wondered what would be expected of them and how they could possibly perform the commission Jesus had given them. In spite of doubts and fears, the mighty power of God became manifest when all of them were filled with the Holy Spirit (Acts 2:1–4).

Paul was called by God to preach to the gentiles. In Paul's missions, he preached the Good News of Christ first to the Jews, but if they rejected him, he went to the gentiles. Paul ran into many conflicts, some from Jews who regarded him as a traitor, some from those who made their living from idol worship, but he also gained many converts.

As Christianity grew, it started to reach many cultures that looked at Christianity from different perspectives.

For the Christian community of converted Jews, religion was primarily a "way of love." God had compassion and tenderness, qualities our culture usually attributes to the feminine. In fact, the Hebrew term for "word"—as in Jesus, the word of God—was feminine in gender. Religion was primarily a life lived in love, and Jesus was the divine model of this way of life.

For the Greek mind, so interested in philosophy, Christianity had to be understood in terms of metaphysics. Jesus was the wisdom of God, a being itself made flesh, and the communicator of divine wisdom. This community placed great emphasis on creeds and dogma.

Rome, with the great tradition of justice and law, gave Christianity an inheritance of morals. Christ was the greatest of all lawgivers. As a result, ethics and morals became central. For these Christians, Jesus was the perfect man. Greeks and Romans had problems reconciling Jesus as human being and Jesus as God.

The early Church also had to contend with discord inside. Many Christians denied their faith to save their lives during the persecution of Christians in the early centuries of the Church. Then when persecution subsided, they would want to return to the Church. The decision over what to do with them divided many Christian communities, although the approved approach was to accept them back as penitents.

The Church was also threatened by heresies, including those who claimed to have secret knowledge of God, and others who believed that the end of the world was at hand. These are issues with which we still struggle today.

Despite persecution and doctrinal wrangling, the life of the Church developed. Converts, after lengthy instruction, were baptized, usually by immersion in a river. The ceremony of the breaking of bread, the Mass, bound the Christian community together in the real flesh and blood of Jesus.

As Christianity grew, it started to reach many cultures that looked at Christianity from different perspectives.

Bishops, who received their power to rule from the apostles, offered sacrifice and directed the Church in their particular locality. If the Christian community was large enough to warrant it, the bishop would ordain presbyters (priests) to assist him. Deacons, besides instructing, saw to the various charities of the Church and distributed the Eucharist.

In 303, Diocletian unleashed perhaps the most frightful persecution that the Church had ever suffered. Thousands of Christians in Asia Minor, Africa, and Greece were mutilated or killed. This persecution lasted through his two successors. Then, in 312, the western emperor, Constantine, who had become a Christian, successfully defeated Diocletian's successor, and in 313 decreed the edict of Milan, granting general religious tolerance in the empire.

HOW We Live It

- *What does Christianity offer to you that you can't find anywhere else?*

- *In what ways are Catholics persecuted for their beliefs today?*

The Church Continues to Grow

Freed from the constant anxiety of persecution, Christians in the fourth century had the leisure to ponder the truths of God's revelation made through Jesus Christ. Many great thinkers—like Saints Ambrose, Basil, and Gregory Nazianzen—expanded the Church's understanding of God.

In the fifth century, the Roman Empire began to collapse as barbarian tribes invaded. At first, Roman Christians were reluctant to have anything to do with their conquerors. Eventually, however, they began to feel the call to convert and civilize the invaders. Many of these missions resulted in mass "conversions" ordered by a newly baptized ruler.

To bring the newly converted to a deeper knowledge of Christianity, monasteries and parishes were founded. The austere life and education of the monks helped instruct the people, while parishes made Christianity the center of community life. Social service was almost completely up to the Church. In rural areas, the monasteries were the center of civilization.

Charlemagne was crowned as holy Roman emperor in 800. He promoted Christianity but renewed the problems of church-state ties. Nobles appointed bishops, often choosing someone who would support their interests rather than the Gospel. Priests were appointed by the local landowners and had little or no training. Those in religious orders became more interested in material possessions and vices than the Gospel.

In the eleventh and early twelfth centuries, Saint Bernard and others brought reform to religious orders, stressing a return to a life of prayer. The same centuries saw the flowering of the great universities, Gothic architecture, and extraordinary scholars like Hildegard of Bingen. She not only ran an abbey but had considerable influence with state and Church leaders.

In 1054, divisions between the East and West led to separation of the Eastern Church from Rome. This was also the time of the Crusades. The motives for these Crusades were not merely, or even mostly, religious, but boredom, greed, and the desire for power.

The highlights of the thirteenth century came from great saints like Saint Francis of Assisi, Saint Clare, Saint Dominic, and Saint Thomas Aquinas. Francis and Dominic changed the way Christianity was preached. Monasteries had been preserving the teachings of the Church, but many had lost contact with the people who would benefit from their learning. Francis and Dominic went out to the people to preach and lived a life of poverty among them.

The fourteenth century brought confusion to the Church when the popes moved from Rome to Avignon in France and when two or three men claimed to be pope at the same time. In the fifteenth century, corruption among many Church leaders and interference by the secular authorities increased. Many saintly Catholics, including Saint Catherine of Siena, called for renewal.

In 1517, Martin Luther, a Catholic monk, called for an end to the abuses in the Church. He wanted reform in the Church, not to break away, but poor communications, stubbornness on both sides, and interference by secular authorities led him to a "protestant" position. Division followed division, and Christianity has since been split into many hundreds of churches.

Social service and everyday spirituality were the focus of the seventeenth and eighteenth centuries. Saint Francis de Sales wrote books that called laypeople to holiness. His good friend, Saint Jane de Chantal, met him when she was a widow raising three children, managing an estate, and caring for an invalid father-in-law.

At the same time a new heresy, Jansenism, appeared. Jansenism is a philosophy that said Jesus died for a select few. It promoted fear of receiving the sacraments or getting close to God. Even after this teaching was condemned by the Church, the spirit of Jansenism continued to be influential. One person who argued against this approach was Saint Alphonsus Liguori. He wrote books for the person in the pew and for theologians trying to revive the love of God in hearts frozen by pessimism.

HOW We Live It

- *What will happen to the Catholic Church in the future? That depends on you. Write down the next part of the Catholic Church's story.*

A Community of Faith

The Second Vatican Council, a gathering in Rome of all the Catholic bishops of the world in the 1960s, restated Catholic beliefs for the modern world and instituted many changes in worship and structure, encouraging Catholics to renew their efforts to follow Christ. The laity were called to new involvement: "It is the special vocation of the laity to seek the kingdom of God by engaging in temporal affairs and directing them according to God's will" (The Dogmatic Constitution of the Church, # 31).

The role of laity is evident not only in the workplace and the home but in the Church, too. Ministries, at one time the exclusive province of the priest, have been properly distributed to the people of God.

Catholic Christians continued to give selflessly of their lives to advance the cause of peace and to end suffering. Dorothy Day, cofounder of the Catholic Worker movement, and Mother Teresa, founder of the Missionaries of Charity in the streets of Calcutta, worked heroically to make God's love vivid to the poor. Dom Helder Camara, Archbishop of Recife and Olinda in Brazil, won a People's Peace Prize for his commitment to the poor.

El Salvador's Archbishop Oscar Romero was shot and killed while celebrating Mass in the cathedral in San Salvador. He is considered a champion of the impoverished of Latin America. Prior to his death he spoke out forcefully on behalf of El Salvador's disenfranchised poor, criticizing the wealthy and powerful for policies and practices that marginalized the indigent.

There are many challenges facing the Church today: materialism, atheism, the effects of new technology, the unstable condition of the international political scene, a shortage of vocations to the priesthood and religious life, just to name a few. And all its members are human, as fallible as the apostles. Yet, the Church is still the body of Christ, and we can trust that he will continue to guide and strengthen the Church.

Saint Paul writes, "So we, who are many, are one body in Christ, and individually we are members one of another. We have gifts that differ according to the grace given to us: prophecy, in proportion to faith" (Romans 12:5–6). Parents raising their children, students attending class, adults at their jobs, priests in their ministries, the elderly in nursing homes…all are the body of Christ.

> *"So we, who are many, are one body in Christ, and individually we are members of one another."*
> ROMANS 12:5

Throughout its history, the Church has been the means through which millions of people in every age, and of every class and every race, have come to know Jesus Christ and his life-giving message. At times in the Church's history some of her members have been unfaithful to the spirit of God. But the spirit always remains faithful to the Church. That's why the Church continues to be a sign of Christ's presence in the world and to proclaim his message of love, forgiveness, dignity, joy, hope, and peace.

HOW We Live It

- *Who is a spiritual role model for you?*

- *As a member of the body of Christ, which "part" are you? Why?*

- *How can you make Christ present in the world through your daily life?*

Conclude the session by reciting the Apostles' Creed:

I believe in God, the Father almighty,
creator of heaven and earth.
I believe in Jesus Christ, his only Son, our Lord.
He was conceived by the power of the Holy Spirit
and born of the Virgin Mary.
He suffered under Pontius Pilate,
was crucified, died, and was buried.
He descended to the dead.
On the third day he rose again.
He ascended into heaven,
and is seated at the right hand of the Father.
He will come again to judge the living
and the dead.
I believe in the Holy Spirit,
the holy catholic Church,
the communion of saints,
the forgiveness of sins,
the resurrection of the body,
and the life everlasting. Amen.

SUGGESTED RESOURCES

Bellitto, Christopher M. *Church History 101: A Concise Overview.*

Himes, Michael J. *The Catholic Church in the 21st Century: Finding Hope for Its Future in the Wisdom of Its Past.*

Miller, Richard W. *Women and the Shaping of Catholicism: Women Through the Ages.*

Vomund, Jeffrey. *What Catholics Believe About the Church* (DVD).

Concluding Prayer: O God, we thank you for the gift of Church. Help us see ourselves as valuable members of the body of Christ, each with unique gifts and talents that we bring to the community of faith. Open our eyes to the beauty of your work in all people and in all places, and grant us the grace to grow in faith and love. Amen.

SESSION 2

What Makes Us Catholic?

WHO'S who in the Church?

WHAT do Catholics believe about their faith and the Church?

WHERE do Catholics go to encounter God?

WHEN does the liturgical year begin and what seasons does it consist of?

WHY do Catholics venerate the crucifix? The tabernacle?

Opening Song: "Earthen Vessels," by the Saint Louis Jesuits, or a hymn of your choice

Opening Prayer: God of all creation, you have called us to this community known as the Catholic Church. Bless our work during this session today, that we may come to better understand who we are and where we come from as members of this Church. Open our minds and our hearts to your word, and to the words of those gathered here with us today. Inspire us with your spirit, and guide us in the way of Jesus, the Christ. Amen.

Reading: John 15:12–17

Spend a moment in quiet reflection.

What Do Catholics Believe?

In the first centuries after Christ, Christians wondered "how God worked." Questions surfaced that were not explained in the New Testament record of Jesus' teachings. People needed answers to such questions as, "How can one God be Father, Son, and Holy Spirit? How can Jesus be both divine and human?"

Many great theological debates, and not a few religious wars, sprang from questions concerning the nature of God. In 325, the bishops gathered at a Council held in the city of Nicaea and adopted the Nicene Creed as the true and orthodox belief of the universal Church.

Every Sunday, Catholics profess their faith by saying the Nicene Creed. We will now read this prayer aloud together.

We believe in one God, the Father, the Almighty,
maker of heaven and earth,
of all that is seen and unseen.
We believe in one Lord, Jesus Christ,
the only Son of God,
eternally begotten of the Father, God from God,
Light from Light, true God from true God,
begotten, not made, one in Being with the Father.
Through him all things were made.
For us men and for our salvation
he came down from heaven:
by the power of the Holy Spirit
he was born of the Virgin Mary, and became man.
For our sake he was crucified under Pontius Pilate;
he suffered, died, and was buried.
On the third day he rose again in fulfillment of the
Scriptures;
he ascended into heaven and is seated at the right
hand of the Father.
He will come again in glory to judge the living and
the dead,
and his kingdom will have no end.
We believe in the Holy Spirit, the Lord,
the giver of life,
who proceeds from the Father and the Son.
With the Father and Son he is worshiped and
glorified.
He has spoken through the Prophets.
We believe in one holy catholic and apostolic
Church.
We acknowledge one baptism for the forgiveness of
sins.
We look for the resurrection of the dead,
and the life of the world to come. Amen.

Read through again, silently.

HOW We Live It

- **What part of this prayer speaks most clearly to you, and why?**

The Liturgical Year

To get better at something, we practice, and it is the same with being Catholic. The practices, rituals, and traditions that are part of our faith reinforce our spiritual growth and help us become more fully present to the spirit of God within us.

Catholics have many traditions that help make ordinary days and special days into celebrations of God's love. Some of these practices relate to the liturgy and the liturgical cycle.

The word "*liturgy*" includes the celebration of all the sacraments as well as the program of psalms and prayers of the Church called the "Liturgy of the Hours." In general, liturgy is the combined activity of God's people, the Church, and the activity of the savior of God's people, Jesus Christ.

The "*liturgical year*" is the Church's way of celebrating and reliving the great events of our salvation. Each year follows a pattern, and prayers for Mass have been organized to fit into it.

The liturgical year begins with the season of *Advent*, which is celebrated during the four weeks immediately preceding Christmas in a spirit of anticipation and waiting for the Messiah. The Church invites us to be aware that, just as Christ grew and matured in Mary's womb, Christ is growing and maturing in our hearts.

December 25 marks the beginning of the *Christmas season*, which includes the solemnity of Mary as the Mother of God on January 1, the celebrations of the Holy Family on the first Sunday after Christmas, and the Epiphany. The Baptism of Our Lord (usually the third Sunday after Christmas) closes out the Christmas season and marks the beginning of Ordinary Time.

Ordinary Time is that time in the yearly cycle that falls outside the seasons of Lent, Easter, Advent, and Christmas. During this time, the mystery of Christ in all its fullness is celebrated and reflected on.

The season of *Lent* begins with *Ash Wednesday*. Lent is a penitential season. Christians perform acts of penance and almsgiving to enlighten and purify their lives in preparation for the celebration of the Easter mysteries. Lent lasts forty days, patterned after Jesus' forty days in the desert, as told in the Gospel of Matthew 4:1–11.

The Easter Triduum is a three-day festival. Holy Thursday celebrates the institution of the holy Eucharist at the Last Supper; Good Friday celebrates Our Lord's passion and death by prayer and required fasting; Holy Saturday is the "vigil" day to prepare for Easter by prayer, reflection, and optional fasting. At sunset, the Church explodes in joy and celebration of Jesus' resurrection.

Easter Sunday morning begins the fifty-day period of celebrating Jesus' resurrection, the hope of our resurrection, the ascension of Jesus into heaven, the life of the Christian until Jesus comes again, and the coming of the Holy Spirit and the birthday of the Church on Pentecost Sunday.

Easter is followed by a long period of *Ordinary Time* that ends just before Advent with Christ the King Sunday, almost another type of "epiphany" celebration that brings us full circle in our celebration of the liturgical year.

All through the liturgical year, a special place is given to Sunday, observed as the Lord's day because Christ rose on the first day of the week. Most major liturgical observances occur on Sunday but there are also special feasts in the liturgical year called holy days of obligation. In the United States, these holy days include the Immaculate Conception (December 8), the Nativity of Our Lord (Christmas, December 25), Mary the Mother of God (January 1), the Ascension of Our Lord (forty days after Easter), the Assumption of the Blessed Virgin Mary (August 15), and All Saints Day (November 1).

HOW We Live It

- *What is your favorite time of year?*
- *What would you celebrate about God during that time of year?*

Inside a Catholic Church

Catholics have many places where they can go to encounter God. One of the primary places is a parish, which the Second Vatican Council said "exists solely for the good of souls."

A parish church has territorial boundaries and serves the needs of the people in its immediate area. Some parishes are not territorial but were built to serve specific groups of immigrants, nationalities, languages, or rites.

Everywhere you look in your parish church there are reminders of God.

The moment you walk in the door you see a bowl of water by the door. This is Holy Water, blessed water used by Catholics to make the sign of the cross as a reminder of their baptism and used in blessings as a sign of God's loving care. The faithful dip their fingers into a small receptacle, sprinkle themselves with the water, and say a prayer or make the sign of the cross.

The altar is the central fixture or table on which the Eucharist is celebrated, itself considered a symbol of Christ. Usually made of precious material, such as stone, marble, or fine wood, it has many different designs, depending on the size and age of the church. During the liturgy, the Communion bread and the cup (chalice) of wine are offered from this table. The book of Mass prayers, called the Sacramentary (Roman Missal), is also used at the altar.

Candles adorn the altar to symbolize Christ's presence and light.

The crucifix is a cross with the image of Jesus on it, representing his suffering and death. It is usually placed in a prominent position near the altar or used processionally at the beginning of a service. The Catholic practice of venerating the crucifix, that is the cross with the figure of Christ, is a declaration of our faith in the total love of God revealed in the death of Christ.

The tabernacle is a specially designated receptacle where the consecrated Eucharist is reserved and venerated. Since Catholics believe that the Eucharist is Christ's body, they believe Jesus is present to us in a real and unique way in the Eucharist. The tabernacle's position in the sanctuary depends on the architecture and the date of the church's construction.

A constantly burning candle, called **the sanctuary lamp**, near the tabernacle, reminds people of Jesus' presence in the Eucharist that is reserved there.

The lectern is the place where the word of God is proclaimed to the congregation during services. The book used for these Scripture readings is called **the Lectionary**.

The Easter, or paschal, candle is a large, ornamented candle symbolic of the risen Christ, which is blessed and lighted during the annual Easter Vigil service and positioned near the altar or lectern. During the Easter season, it burns at every liturgy. After the Easter season, the candle is placed near the baptismal font to symbolize our entering into the death and resurrection of Christ at our baptism. It is also placed next to the casket during the Christian burial service to symbolize that the dead person now shares fully in Christ's redemptive love.

A **baptismal font** is a vessel or basin (mounted on a pedestal) in which water is contained for baptizing. In older churches, the baptismal font was fixed in a room or area in the rear of the church. In newer churches, it is found in a prominent place near or in the sanctuary. In churches where baptism is performed by immersion, there is a pool of water for this purpose.

The reconciliation room or confessional is a small room so arranged that a person can seek counsel or sacramental forgiveness from a priest either face-to-face or anonymously, depending on the choice of the person. The reconciliation room is a precious reminder to Catholics of God's infinite mercy and forgiveness.

HOW We Live It

- *What do the signs and symbols in a Catholic Church say to you about your faith?*

- *What are some places other than your parish that are holy for you, and why?*

Who's Who in the Church

Who is the pope and what effect does he have on your life? What is the average person's place in the Church? In this session, we will discuss some of these people. These are only brief descriptions. You will learn more as you meet some of these people and read more about them.

Let's start at the top. Christ is the head of the Church. From him, "the whole body, nourished and held together by its ligaments and sinews, grows with a growth that is from God" (Colossians 2:19). Jesus gave some of his disciples special authority, however, to continue his mission, and Catholics believe this authority has been passed down through the centuries.

The pope is the recognized leader of the Catholic Church on earth. Acting in union with all the bishops of the world, the pope preserves and spreads Christ's teaching as embodied in Catholic understanding of Scripture, the traditions of the Church through history, and the unfolding understanding of divine revelation. The pope also inherits the Apostle Peter's responsibility to serve the whole Church and the faith that has been handed down.

The Catholic Church teaches that the commissions Jesus gave to the apostles were passed down to successors through the ages to the present day. Catholics call the successors of the apostles "bishops." The **bishop** is the chief pastor and head of a specific diocese. He has charge of all matters of Church life within the designated boundaries of his diocese. In a large diocese, the bishop is aided by auxiliary bishop(s) who assist with the sacramental and administrative duties of a bishop.

An **archbishop** is a bishop who heads an important ecclesiastical post or heads a diocese ranked an archdiocese because of its significance in Catholic history or population. The papal nuncio is an archbishop who acts as the official Vatican delegate to a country. He holds the rank of ambassador. In the United States and Canada, he also functions as a facilitator between these countries' bishops and the Vatican offices in Rome.

Cardinal is an important honorary rank bestowed upon members of the clergy by the pope. Until he reaches the age of 80, a cardinal is allowed to vote in the election of a new pope.

Throughout his ministry, Jesus gave his apostles special commissions and commands. And after his resurrection, he said, "Go, therefore, and make disciples of all nations, baptizing them in the name of the Father, and of the Son, and of the Holy Spirit, and teaching them to observe all that I have commanded you" (Matthew 28:19–20). That's why the bishops have ordained priests to be their coworkers in this mission and have handed down some of their ministerial role to them. The priest can be a **diocesan priest** or religious priest. A diocesan priest is attached to a specific diocese, under the authority of the local bishop. A **religious priest** is a member of a religious community and works in many different parts of the world at the invitation of local bishops.

The **pastor** is the bishop's direct representative in the pastoral care of a parish church. The other appointed priests in the parish are called "associate pastors" or "parochial vicars." According to the *Code of Canon Law*, "The pastor is the proper shepherd of the parish entrusted to him…he carries out for his community the duties of teaching, sanctifying, and governing, with the cooperation of other presbyters or deacons and the assistance of lay members of the Christian faithful" (Canon 519).

A **deacon** is an ordained member of the clergy, ranked under bishops and priests. A deacon can either be transitional (a step taken while studying for the priesthood) or permanent (ordained only for the diaconate). Only permanent deacons may be married, and only if they were married at the time of their ordination. If their wives die, they cannot remarry. The deacon's ministry is performing pastoral works of charity and assisting in liturgical functions.

In the Catholic Church, a **religious** is someone who belongs to a religious institute or order. Each institute has a specific ministry, like prayer, service to the poor, teaching, and so forth. Some communities are the Order of Friars Minor (Franciscans), the Society of Jesus (Jesuits), and the Congregation of the Most Holy Redeemer (Redemptorists), which publishes this workbook. Religious take vows of poverty, chastity, and obedience in order to follow Christ more faithfully.

People commonly use the word nun to describe all women in religious orders. Actually, you should use the word "**sister**." A nun is a sister who belongs to an order that is "enclosed." Nuns reside in convents and have limited contact with the world. A **brother** is a non-ordained member of a religious order of men. Priests and brothers in monastic orders are referred to as "monks." Religious communities can also include laypersons, deacons, priests, and bishops.

The **laity** of the Church are called to be disciples of Christ in the same way. All baptized Catholics who are not members of the clergy are considered laity. Laypeople are called to exercise their baptism by bringing the presence of Christ to their life in the world and attaining holiness by fulfilling their own particular duties in life.

HOW We Live It

- *What are some of the ministries within a parish?*
- *Where do you see yourself as a minister in the Church, and why?*

Conclude the session by praying the Lord's Prayer:

Our Father, who art in heaven,
hallowed be thy name.
Thy kingdom come;
thy will be done on earth as it is in heaven.
Give us this day our daily bread,
and forgive us our trespasses
as we forgive those who trespass against us.
And lead us not into temptation,
but deliver us from evil.
Amen.

SUGGESTED RESOURCES

Chittister, Joan. *In Search Of Belief: Revised Edition.*

Davidson, James D. *Catholicism in Motion: The Church in American Society.*

Miller, Richard W., Editor. *Lay Ministry in the Catholic Church: Visioning Church Ministry Through the Wisdom of the Past.*

Redemptorist Fathers. *Handbook for Today's Catholic: Revised Edition.*

Concluding Prayer: O God, we thank you for the gift of Church. Help us see ourselves as valuable members of the body of Christ, each with unique gifts and talents that we bring to the community of faith. Open our eyes to the beauty of your work in all people and in all places, and grant us the grace to grow in faith and love. Amen.

SESSION 3

Growing in Faith

FROM whom do we receive the gifts that we need to reach out and minister to others?

WHAT is faith and what does it mean to live by faith?

WHERE can we turn to intensify our search for understanding of our faith?

WHEN do I experience feelings of guilt, and how do I overcome them?

WHY is faith an important aspect of daily life?

Opening Song: "Eye Has Not Seen," by Marty Haugen, or a hymn of your choice

Opening Prayer: God of all creation, you have called us to this community known as the Catholic Church. Bless our work during this session today, that we may come to better understand who we are and where we come from as members of this Church. Open our minds and our hearts to your word, and to the words of those gathered here with us today. Inspire us with your spirit, and guide us in the way of Jesus, the Christ. Amen.

Reading: James 2:14–19, 26

Spend a moment in quiet reflection.

Your Journey of Faith

It would be impossible for us to live without faith. We have faith that the people who prepare our food will not poison us, and motorists will stay on their side of the road.

Most of our knowledge is based on faith. Saint Augustine said, "I began to consider the countless things I believed that I had not seen, or that had happened with me not there—so many things in the history of nations, so many facts about places and cities that I had never seen, so many things told me by friends, by doctors, by this person, by that person: and unless we accepted these things, we could do nothing at all in this life."

Living by faith means that we live as though we are loved and desired by God, even when our life experiences seem to fly in the face of this conviction. No matter what anyone says, we hold fast to our conviction that nothing can separate us from the love of God (Romans 8:35–39).

Faith introduces us to a kind of knowledge that human intelligence alone cannot attain. God's message to us is quite simple: "I love you. Will you let me love you that you may learn to love?" When other people tell us, "I love you," we encounter the same invitation. We can look for signs of the reality of their love, but we cannot prove that they love us in the same way we can show that two plus two equals four.

The only way to know their love is to enter it—to open ourselves to being touched by them. This is how it is with God. Faith enables us to receive God's love, which in turn places within us a new understanding of love and life. God is as close to us when we are dry and cranky as when we are filled with joy and exuberance. Simply persisting in the struggle to learn and love is our most authentic expression of faith.

For most of us, the beginning of faith is not dramatic. A small seed of faith is planted in whatever good soil may be found in our hearts. Then it grows by being watered and cared for daily. Faith is a process, the most important process of all because it leads us to God.

For most of us, the beginning of faith is not dramatic.

The more we learn about faith and the more we live our faith, the closer we get to God.

Does faith mean we don't question? Some people might think this means that they should accept whatever they are told without questioning it. But faith does not mean that we have all the answers; it means believing God has the answers.

It would be virtually impossible for a thinking, active Catholic to go through life without questions and doubts. It's part of the faith process. Jesus didn't abandon the apostles because they had doubts or because they couldn't understand everything right away.

Faith thrusts us into a lifelong and ongoing relationship with God. Even people engaged in deep, intimate human relationships wonder at times. But a couple can actually grow closer, their love deeper and more mature, after struggling through their doubts. Likewise, our doubts can be a catalyst to a deeper relationship and closer union with God.

During a time of struggle with doubts, we can intensify our search for understanding through prayer, reading, reception of the sacraments, counseling, and good works. God may not always give us the answers we want to hear but, if we are to grow in faith, we must keep searching and exploring God's revelation. True faith is never anti-intellectual; true faith makes full use of reason, imagination, memory, feeling, and will.

Faith is a gift of God, but our work is to remain open to receiving that gift and to use the gift in our lives. This is harder than it sounds. Trying to be in control of our own lives, selfishness, and anxiety are some things that can close us off from this gift.

HOW We Live It

- *Think of something that you're trying very hard to control in your life. It could be a person, a situation, anything. Now think of one small thing about this situation that you can give up and turn over to God.*

- *What does your lifestyle say about what you believe?*

Conversion Begins a Maturing in Faith

The word "conversion" has several layers of meaning. At its root, it means "to change or turn around." Its most common usage describes the process of changing religions.

While this is true, conversion is also the ever-present call of the already committed Christian to grow both in the faith and in the living of it. It means deepening our relationship with God and our fellow Christians.

The first step in the conversion process is to turn to Jesus Christ, accepting him as Lord and Savior, and choosing to live the life of faith in the community of God's faithful people. This first turning is called "initial conversion." It may be a moving experience, a dramatic moment that turns a person completely about-face. It may jar a person to the very depth of being.

But that's just the beginning. The initial conversion needs time, space, and opportunity to sink roots into the rich soil of a person's life. Conversion also requires perseverance, the gradual and continual redirecting of our lives. It is like fine-tuning a television picture that is already good but could be better. Ongoing conversion means steering our lives, day by day, closer to God.

One of the most profound conversion stories in the Gospel is the account of Jesus' transfiguration (Matthew 17:1–9), where he takes Peter, James, and John to the top of a mountain and they see Jesus for who he is: God's Son. The experience is so intense for Peter and the others that they want to stay there forever. But they had to come down off the mountain and get back to the daily grind of things.

Even if the apostles' "peak" experience didn't last very long, that didn't mean the apostles left the presence of God or were distant from God (or God from them). They continued to walk with Jesus, even though the special feelings and emotions of that experience soon faded in the reality of Jesus' suffering and death.

It is not our nature to be in a high state of religious experience all the time. The journey of faith involves living and believing as a Christian, even—or especially—at those times when we don't feel like it. But there are moments when we need to be reassured that God is with us.

This is where the Church can play an important part in our lives. Prayer, hearing and reading God's word, going to Mass, receiving the sacraments—especially the sacrament of reconciliation—and getting spiritual direction can help us realize God's daily presence in our lives.

Conversion is a lifelong process. It encompasses the stages of development we naturally go through while growing to adulthood with all the inherent twists and turns, ups and downs of a life journey. It means becoming progressively more open to God's presence in our lives, more sensitive and responsive to the needs of others, more desirous to see God's kingdom of peace and justice in our world.

Conversions occur in ordinary circumstances, too—a meeting with a stranger, a wedding or a funeral, a visit to a church or a hospital. Simple things like putting up with an irritating neighbor or in-law can be a moment of grace.

We will be changed to the degree that we respond to our call to conversion. We can ignore the grace or we can respond totally. It is not God's initiative that is lacking. We are chased "down the nights and down the days" as described in Francis Thompson's poem "The Hound of Heaven."

Call on God's help. Look at your life. The grace of conversion has touched you and will call you even further. Your life in God is one of "continued conversion." Respond with all your heart.

HOW We Live It

- *What are your expectations of Jesus and the Church? Do any of these need to go through a change?*

- *What activities and changes might help you in your conversion process?*

- *Think about a recent "ordinary experience" that was a moment of conversion for you.*
  How did you respond to this call to conversion? What part of you was converted?

Take a Look Inside

Our spiritual longing is part of our nature. It usually manifests itself in the search for meaning, or more specifically, in the many kinds of pursuits we use in an attempt to complete ourselves. Food, money, alcohol, romantic love, status, and friendships all bring temporary gratification to our spiritual needs, but then these pursuits leave us hungering for more.

As conversion takes root in our lives, we may find it necessary to leave certain aspects of our life behind, to scrutinize our patterns and behaviors and consider which actions bring us closer to God and which close us off from God's love. When we scrutinize something, we look at it carefully, examining it thoroughly. We look within ourselves to find anything that keeps us from God. Then we look to God to heal those weaknesses and strengthen us to face further temptations.

Breaking out of selfish habits can be a very painful growth process, and we would rather not experience the suffering that accompanies growth. Living a life of faith, however, means becoming a disciple of Christ. Faith enables us to live a life of love in a world that all too often shows itself to be callous and resistant to the ways of love.

Looking closely at our lives can make us aware of our shortcomings and failures. It can leave us with feelings of guilt for choices and actions that were less than desirable. Guilt, on the most obvious level, follows having done something wrong, something hurtful to another person, something that violates the commandments. When our acts or decisions are morally unacceptable, we may feel guilty.

The universal human sense of guilt can remind us of our vulnerability.

For some time, there has been a psychological notion that guilt is harmful and should be gotten rid of or ignored. It can be regarded as unhealthy to feel remorse over anything. But when we feel guilty, it's often because we have done something we shouldn't have. On this level, guilt can be reasonable and healthy. It is a sign that our conscience is working.

Another level of guilt comes from violating standards of action that we have made on our own or may even have invented: "should–itis." It can read like this: "I feel I should always prove capable; I should never make a mistake; I should use every moment of time; I should never express certain feelings; I should be able to do everything I read about; I should"...the list can be very long. This kind of guilt generally has little use in nurturing a relationship with God.

A third level of guilt is universal. It runs like an underground stream beneath our living; and only at times does it surface into feeling. This guilt comes from that deep, inner part of us that recognizes that we have somehow gone away from God. It is our half-conscious awareness of the human difficulty involved in original sin. We are made for God, yet we don't live for God and in God. The result is underlying guilt.

The universal human sense of guilt can remind us of our vulnerability. We are not able to do anything or become anyone on our own; we are completely dependent on God's mercy. The more aware we are of our vulnerability, the more we love God and the more God can help us find peace with our guilt.

Here are some steps we may go through in ordering our lives to be open to receiving the gift of faith:

We recognize the folly of trying to fulfill ourselves through selfish pursuits and behaviors. We know this through the hopelessness and sense of guilt that our ways leave within us.

We believe that God wants us to know him. Christ stands at the door of the human spirit and knocks, ready to come in and live with us, but waiting patiently for our invitation (see Revelation 3:20).

We ask God to forgive us and make God's home within us. We plead that God's spirit will form our own spirits in God's way (see 1 Corinthians 2:10–16).

Some people cling to their guilt. They'd rather keep it than face it. This is an evasion of responsibility for their lives and is very destructive. Nothing can be done to heal my guilt and bring me to peace until I am ready to see it and decide to make tomorrow different. Guilt cries out for change—for conversion.

HOW We Live It

- *To what extent is my life God-centered? Other-centered? Self-centered?*

- *What are some of the "should haves" in my life? How do these keep me from being a faithful disciple of Christ?*

- *What actions can I take to reconcile feelings of guilt in my life and move toward a more loving relationship with God?*

Discovering Our Gifts and Abilities

Now there are varieties of gifts, but the same Spirit; and there are varieties of services, but the same Lord; and there are varieties of activities, but it is the same God who activates all of them in everyone. To each is given the manifestation of the Spirit for the common good" (1 Corinthians 12:4–7).

As we continue in our process of conversion and move toward reconciliation with our past, we look ahead to our own unique gifts and abilities, and how these can be used for the greater good. Saint Paul tells us that gifts are not given to us for our enjoyment and pleasure, but for the benefit of others. So, the question is not just what gifts you have, but how you use them to minister to others.

Perhaps you can recognize some of these gifts as your own.

Wisdom

It is said that "wisdom" comes with age, as it often does. But this is by no means automatic. Wisdom is a gift of the Holy Spirit. It is attained through having an open mind, learning from experience, knowing human nature, knowing that God is alive and active at the heart of our world. Knowing there is a meaning to life is part of the wisdom we receive from God. And it changes the way we live.

Knowledge

We may not have graduate degrees but we all have knowledge we can share with others. The important thing is not how much knowledge you have but whether your expression of it is done with compassion.

Healing

When we think of healing, we may think of miraculous returns of physical health or the work done by professionals like nurses and doctors. It would be easy for most of us to say we don't have those gifts of healing. But anything we do to lift a depressed spirit, to make a sad face smile, to touch a hurting heart is also healing.

Mighty deeds

We tend to think of mighty deeds in terms of ourselves—what will make us look powerful in the eyes of others. We want to be in charge of a big project, we want to bring in huge numbers of people for a parish program. We want to have people do what we tell them. But if we think of mighty deeds in terms of others, we realize that what has the most powerful effect on people is not the big spectacular show, but the humble, thoughtful service that no one else will do.

Prophecy

Prophecy for the Christian is not foretelling the future. Prophecy is living according to God's values and announcing them in situations where they do not appear to be present. Dorothy Day, cofounder of the Catholic Worker community, saw injustice in the way the poor were treated in this country, and she labored to change that reality. She sought dignity and respect as she helped meet the basic needs of the poor and disenfranchised.

Discernment of spirits

It is easy to write off someone who is hostile, critical, or who just doesn't agree with us. But those who discern spirits see that everyone is a child of God with gifts to share. Discernment of spirits requires looking at situations from God's perspective and asking ourselves not just what we want but what God would want us to do.

The gift of tongues

After the Holy Spirit descended at Pentecost, Peter and the other apostles were able to speak so that people from every land could understand. They were able to communicate God's Good News to everyone. Though often the gift of speaking in tongues refers to a specific phenomenon, we would like to extend that meaning to speaking the language of the Holy Spirit. This language is love and compassion. We communicate this when we speak up about the good in others, give credit and appreciation for service, and express our admiration and encouragement.

Interpretation of tongues

When we truly listen to others we are able to understand that what they need may lie deeper than the surface of their words. When someone really listens without making judgments or giving advice, people feel they are accepted and welcomed as they are. It's one of the simplest ministries, but often the most difficult.

HOW We Live It

- *Do you resonate with any of the gifts of the spirit listed above?*

- *Are there other gifts and talents that you can use to serve others?*

- *How have others' gifts helped you to grow in faith? Is there someone in particular who is helping you right now? In what way?*

Conclude the session with this Prayer of Redemption:

*God of all creation, you rebuild what is broken
and restore what has fallen into disrepair.
Take my life into your hands.
Breathe your Holy Spirit into me.
Re-create me. Restore me to yourself.
Make me new and keep me yours. Amen.*

SUGGESTED RESOURCES

Deeley, Mary Katharine. *Mothers, Lovers, Priests, Prophets, and Kings: What the Old Testament Tells Us About God and Ourselves.*

Sullivan, Joseph T. *How to Share Your Faith With Others: A Good News Guidebook.*

Torrens, James S. *Dare to Commit: Say Yes in a World of Maybe.*

Winninger, Thomas J. *Get Out of the Boat: Discover the Meaning of Your Life.*

Concluding Prayer: O God, we thank you for the gift of Church. Help us see ourselves as valuable members of the body of Christ, each with unique gifts and talents that we bring to the community of faith. Open our eyes to the beauty of your work in all people and in all places, and grant us the grace to grow in faith and love. Amen.

Notes

SESSION

4

Scripture

WHO are some of the key people/figures in the Old Testament?

WHAT does it mean to say that the Bible is inspired by God?

WHERE in the Bible do the different readings come from that we proclaim at Mass?

WHEN was the Bible written?

WHY is reading the Bible important?

Opening Song: "Faith of Our Fathers," or a hymn of your choice

Opening Prayer: O God, may your words remain with me, in my mind, on my lips, and in my heart. Dancing before my sorrow or joy, may their message of love not depart. For every joy has been written, and every sorrow has been consoled by your holy word, forever preserved, as each chapter and verse unfold.

Reading: Matthew 7:24–28

Spend a moment in quiet reflection.

A Book for All Seasons

The Bible is a collection of writings about God, about God's relationship with humankind, about our relationship with God, and about how God wants people to relate to one another.

The word "bible" comes from a Greek word that means "books." Many different people, under the inspiration of the Holy Spirit, wrote the books of the Bible in different times and places, over a period of about one thousand years—from about 900 BC to AD 100.

When we say the Bible is inspired by God, it means God chose certain people who made use of their abilities with the Holy Spirit acting in them and through them. God did not dictate the Bible word for word. In a biblical context, the word "testament" means "agreement" or "covenant." The Old Testament is a collection of books about the covenant between God and our Jewish ancestors in the faith.

There are forty-six books in **the Catholic Old Testament**. (The Protestant Old Testament has thirty-nine, a break that happened during the Reformation.) These books can be grouped into segments that help us better understand the journey of God's people.

The Torah, or Law, includes the first five books of the Old Testament, also known as the Pentateuch ("five books" in Greek). It tells of the most important journey of all—the journey of the Israelites to become the people of God through Abraham's path to Canaan and the Israelites' exodus from Egypt.

The Historical Books cover the period from the entry of the Israelites into the Promised Land about 1225 BC to the end of the Maccabean wars about 135 BC. The Israelites' view of world events sees God's guiding hand in everything.

The Wisdom Books are an inspired search into the meaning of life. The authors use poetry and proverbs, sayings and songs, and they face the problems of our origin and destiny, of human suffering, good and evil, right and wrong.

The Prophetic Books are not writings that foretell the future but are the words of those who speak for God about situations that were contemporary to them.

The books of the New Testament are about the covenant between God through Jesus and God's people. The New Testament is a fulfillment and continuation of the covenant of the Old Testament.

For twenty years after the resurrection of Jesus, missionaries spread the good news of Jesus by preaching. Eventually Christians began to feel a need to preserve their heritage in writing. Collections of the sayings of Jesus, liturgical prayers, and professions of faith began to appear.

Most of the twenty-seven New Testament books were written by the end of the first century. Each book reveals a different side of Jesus. The four Gospels record the words and deeds of Jesus as they were remembered and handed down in the early generations of the Church.

The books of the New Testament can be grouped this way:

Four Gospels—different Gospels were written for different communities. The Gospel of Mark tells about the public ministry and the humanity of Jesus. The Gospel of Matthew focuses on the teachings of Jesus. The Gospel of Luke reveals Jesus' concern for the poor and for women. The Gospel of John leads us into the mystery of Jesus.

Acts of the Apostles—an account of how the early Church lived and grew.

Thirteen epistles, or letters, of Saint Paul or Paul's followers.

Eight epistles, or letters, of other apostles.

The Book of Revelation—a message of hope for persecuted Christians, promising Christ's ultimate triumph in history—not a tract predicting the future.

The New Testament writings tell not who Jesus *was* but who he *is*. More than mere historical documents, these writings have the power to change your life.

HOW We Live It

- *How well do you know the Bible? Have you taken time to read it, or is it still a mystery to you?*

- *Describe a covenant between you and God. How does that agreement affect your life?*

The People of God

In the Old Testament, we find a narrative of God's relationships with God's people—the awakening of their awareness, their flights from or their journeys toward God. In these ancient stories, we can recognize our own because to seek God and meaning in life is as old as humankind.

After Adam and Eve were expelled from Eden, humanity's mind wandered very far from God. As generation passed on to generation, God slipped from the conscious thought of the people. Only a few were left who recognized God's presence in their lives.

Among those few was a man called Abram. One day God said to Abram, "Abram, take your wife, Sarai, and go to a place that I will show you." Abram and Sarai packed up their belongings and traveled many miles to the land called Canaan. Here God gave Abram and Sarai new names: Abraham, which means "father of many nations," and Sarah, "which means princess of the people."

Abraham and Sarah had a son, Isaac, who with his wife Rebekah, bore Jacob, who eventually fathered the leaders of the Twelve Tribes of Israel.

The second-youngest of Jacob's sons, Joseph, was sold by his brothers to merchants traveling to Egypt, where he became a slave in Pharaoh's court. God had given Joseph a gift for interpreting dreams, and when he interpreted Pharaoh's troublesome dreams, the powerful ruler of Egypt made Joseph second ruler in Egypt.

After a time, Joseph reconciled with his brothers and sent for his father, and the family of Israel settled down in Egypt.

For a while, things went well for the descendants of Israel in Egypt. Generations passed, the people multiplied and knew the kindness of their God. But another Pharaoh sensed danger in allowing their numbers to grow and thrive. During this time, Moses came into the history of the Israelites.

God gave Moses a mission—to go to Egypt and tell the Pharaoh to free his people. Although Moses finally agreed to see Pharaoh and demand that the people be released, and although God had promised to help him on this mission, freedom did not come overnight.

For forty years, the Israelites wandered in the wilderness. This journey was a story of promises made and broken, a story of God's faithfulness in the face of the people's unfaithfulness. When at last the Israelites reached the Promised Land, the relationship between God and the people had become a vital part of their worship and their history.

After Moses, people began to see their sojourn as a corporate or "community" journey. God was to be the head of this community. But when the people continued to stray, God sent women and men "judges" to rule them.

Then, the people begged God to send a king, even after God warned them that a king would not be as lenient or generous as God. The first king, Saul, grew jealous of the popularity of a young shepherd boy, David, who had been chosen by God to lead the Israelites. David had many chances to kill Saul but refused to hurt him.

When David was finally proclaimed king, he led his people to years of prosperity. God promised that his kingdom would never end and that one of David's descendants "will be a son to me." Catholics believe God is referring to David's descendant, Jesus.

David's son, Solomon, turned Israel into a powerful nation and built the first temple in Jerusalem. But when Solomon became too attached to the world, he lost touch with God and started worshiping other gods. After Solomon's death and as a result of his turning away from God, the kingdom split into Israel in the north and Judah in the south. These two kingdoms often warred against each other and continued to worship idols.

Many prophets warned of serious religious and political consequences if the people failed to reform and return to living the covenant made with God. The prophets also pleaded with God to give the people more chances, but the Israelites continued to turn away from God.

In 587 BC, just as the prophets had warned, the Babylonians captured Jerusalem and Judah and many of

> *For a while, things went well for the descendants of Israel in Egypt.*

the inhabitants were sent into exile. During this time, a small number, called a remnant, remained faithful and began to hope for the time when they would be reconciled to God again and the glory of King David's reign would return.

When Cyrus conquered Babylon, God inspired him to let the Israelites return to their land and rebuild their temple. This restoration period lasted two hundred years—until the Israelites were conquered by Alexander the Great. After that, except for twenty years of revolt recorded in the Book of Maccabees, the Israelites lived under foreign domination hoping for deliverance.

From 63 BC, the Roman Empire extended its control over the region. They permitted the temple in Jerusalem to be rebuilt in modest proportions. The expectation of reconciliation with God hoped for in days past reached a new fever pitch with the desert prophet, John the Baptist, who announced the imminent coming of the Messiah and baptized Jesus in the Jordan.

In the faith of Christians, Jesus was the one who fulfilled God's promise to Adam and Eve, and the one who restored David's kingdom—but in a new and different glory.

HOW We Live It

- *Some of the Israelites misused the gifts that God had given them. Can you think of a time when you have used a talent or gift from God for selfish ends?*

- *When has it taken a long time or many interventions from God before you secured freedom?*

How Do Catholics Interpret the Bible?

Those who wrote the Bible were addressing the people of their own time and culture. The writer and the reader shared the same mental picture, a picture that may be quite different to today's reader. We need to learn the meaning of each book and the intent of its author, and take into account the living tradition of the whole Church.

The Bible covers the whole spectrum of literary forms familiar to us, plus a few that are unique to the culture of the people who lived in biblical times. There are historical expositions, national epics, stories and parables, poems and liturgical hymns, law codes, letters, wisdom writing, prophecies, teachings, and a wide variety of prayers.

Each mode of expression, each genre, has its own kind of truth. Identify the genre and you are well on your way to understanding the message God is communicating through human words. On the other hand, to be mistaken about the literary form of a biblical passage is tantamount to making it deviate from its true intention.

Consider our modern understanding of the origin of the universe and the evolution of life. Compare that with what we find in the Book of Genesis. The author of the Book of Genesis was not trying to compose a scientific treatise or outline a chronological table. The writer had more important work to do.

So, the writer borrowed a creation story from well-known pagan epics and then significantly revised it to emphasize ancient Israel's unique beliefs. Unlike pagan counterparts, the biblical God did not have to fight adversaries to gain power. The world sprang into existence at God's word of command. Instead of an earth filled with evil powers threatening destruction, absolutely everything created is very good.

Thus, the literary form of Genesis is not a scientific description but a profession of faith in the goodness of God and God's creation. Once this is recognized, we don't have to be upset that the Bible has light existing for three days before the creation of the sun, the moon, and the stars.

The Dogmatic Constitution on Divine Revelation, one of the documents of the Second Vatican Council, tells us, "The Book of Scripture must be acknowledged as teaching firmly, faithfully, and without error that truth that God wanted put into the sacred writings for the sake of our salvation." In other words, the truths to be defended as inerrant concern everything we need to know in order to be saved.

Catholics are fortunate to have this authoritative interpretation of biblical inerrancy. It makes it possible to accept scientific theories and conclusions of historical research without fear of contradicting God's word.

Many devout, sincere lovers of the Bible find themselves greatly disturbed when they come across passages in the Bible that just don't seem to fit with everything else they believe. They find parts of the Bible that contradict the developed faith we live today. That's why the teachings of the Church are so important. The Church makes sure we will not have a mistaken notion of what God wishes us to know.

Catholics enjoy great freedom in interpreting the Bible. In fact, Pius XII and the Council Fathers urged Catholic scholars to grapple with the difficult problems. The Church confidently trusts that the one and same Holy Spirit, who inspired all who wrote and assembled the Bible, continues to guide and direct it in every generation.

"Faith seeking understanding" has been the motto of Christian scholarship from the beginning.

HOW We Live It

- *Name a favorite custom or tradition of yours. How could this be misinterpreted by someone from another place or time?*

- *Do you have a favorite passage of the Bible? Is there an area of Scripture that has confused you in the past? Why?*

- *Sometimes, people feel that the Bible isn't really "theirs." Suggestions have been made that underlining favorite passages or writing your thoughts in the margins can help make your Bible "yours." Can you think of other suggestions?*

Coming to Love the Word of God in Liturgy

Above all, Catholics consider reading the Bible very important because it is the word of God, a message from someone who loves us very much and wants to tell us so. There are many ways we can find help with interpreting this message. One of the most important is during the Liturgy of the Word at Mass.

When the Bible is read and preached in the community of faithful (the Church), those who listen with attention and reverence can come to know the will of God for their lives. They come into personal contact with God who, through the Bible, communicates to them. The Liturgy of the Word is God speaking to us.

At Mass, Catholics remember what Jesus did at the Last Supper. The words of Jesus, "Do this in remembrance of me," have been obeyed without interruption for nearly two thousand years. Every time Catholics gather for Mass, they know they are there to do what Jesus commanded. And they believe that Jesus is made present for them in that action.

The Liturgy of the Word is like an ongoing Bible study. The readings for Sundays have been arranged in such a way that almost all of the New Testament and a varied selection of texts from the Old Testament will have been read over a three-year period. A new cycle starts with every Advent. The Gospel reading in year A is generally from Matthew, in year B from Mark, and in year C from Luke. The Gospel of John is usually read during Easter, Christmas, and to fill out year B because the Gospel of Mark is short.

The first Scripture reading is always taken from the books of the Old Testament except during the Easter season. In general, this reading tells us how God has acted in the past for God's Chosen People. It is usually chosen to relate to the Gospel reading.

The Liturgy of the Word is like an ongoing Bible study.

The responsorial psalm follows the first reading. The psalms were originally composed as prayers to God; they are sometimes attributed to King David. In the first reading, God has spoken to us and now, with the psalm, we participate in prayerful dialogue with God.

The second reading is taken from the writings of Paul or one of the other letters of the New Testament. This reading, however, does not always directly relate to the first reading or the Gospel. Its purpose is to offer us a continuing exposure to these important writings.

The Gospel, because it contains the words of Jesus himself, is always singled out with marks of honor. The Alleluia verse before the Gospel (or the acclamation during Lent) is meant to emphasize Jesus' presence in the word of God.

The homily that follows the Gospel continues to proclaim what we have heard in the Scriptures: the Good News that Jesus is not history, but he is now. A homily has a specific task: to tell us what is happening in Scripture and how it applies to us today.

As listeners we sometimes anticipate a marvelous word that will turn our world upside down. If all our expectation is invested in the preacher, then we risk overlooking the one person who is able to change our lives forever.

That person is Christ. Christ comes, in his own words, "even as you listen." Our attitude is essential. Be actively involved in listening to both the Gospel and the homily; be hungry for Christ's vision and call.

HOW We Live It

- *Do you have a favorite Gospel reading? What does it say to you about Jesus, and why is it appealing?*

- *What is the highlight of the Mass for you? Do you find yourself nourished by the liturgy? Why or why not?*

Conclude the session with this Prayer for Reading the Bible:

O God, may your words remain with me,
in my mind, on my lips, and in my heart.
Dancing before my sorrow or joy,
may their message of love not depart.
For every joy has been written,
and every sorrow has been consoled
by your holy Word, forever preserved,
as each chapter and verse unfold. Amen.

SUGGESTED RESOURCES

Daley, John I.C. *Getting to Know the Bible.*

Parker, William J. *Scripture 101: An Intro to Reading the Bible.*

Redemptorist Fathers. *An Introduction to Scripture for Catholics.*

Concluding Prayer: O God, we thank you for the gift of Church. Help us see ourselves as valuable members of the body of Christ, each with unique gifts and talents that we bring to the community of faith. Open our eyes to the beauty of your work in all people and in all places, and grant us the grace to grow in faith and love. Amen.

Notes

SESSION 5

Jesus Christ

WHO is at the center of Catholic faith and the fruit of Mary's womb?

WHAT do we mean when we say that Jesus "reveals" God to us?

WHERE do Catholics believe that all power, love, healing, and graces come from?

WHEN did the tradition of honoring the saints begin?

WHY do we show honor and respect to Jesus' mother, Mary?

Opening Song: "Jesus, the Lord," by Roc O'Connor, SJ, or a hymn of your choice

Opening Prayer: God of all creation, you have called us to this community known as the Catholic Church. Bless our work during this session today that we may come to better understand who we are and where we come from as members of this Church. Open our minds and our hearts to your word, and to the words of those gathered here with us today. Inspire us with your spirit, and guide us in the way of Jesus, the Christ. Amen.

Reading: Mark 8:27–30

Spend a moment in quiet reflection.

Who Is Jesus Christ?

The Catholic faith is made up of different doctrines and beliefs. We can think about each doctrine of our faith separately, but none of our beliefs can stand alone. Each is related to all the others so that, together, they make up a complete picture. And the picture they form is a picture of Christ.

Jesus Christ alone gives meaning to our faith. He is its living center. Our faith is in the living person of Jesus Christ. Jesus is no ordinary person. Historical research has established the approximate date of his birth, the place, and so on. But these details do not explain why today more than two billion people around the globe call themselves Christians—followers of Christ.

The research does not explain why, thousands of years after his death, Jesus continues to influence the daily lives of so many people. In the history of the world, he stands out as a unique person. And because there has never been anyone like him, we find it impossible to describe him.

Only Jesus himself can reveal the secret of his person. We must, if we are to understand him, let Jesus speak for himself.

How does Jesus describe himself? There are several key passages in John's Gospel that answer this question: John 6:48, John 11:25, John 8:12, John 4:25–26, John 10:14–15 and John 15:1.

Jesus also described himself as "the way, and the truth, and the life" (John 14:6). If we examine this statement carefully, we can learn a great deal about Jesus of Nazareth, God-made-human.

Jesus is the Way

"Where are you from?" is a question we often ask when we meet someone for the first time. It was precisely this question about Jesus that most puzzled everyone who met him: "Can anything good come out of Nazareth?" (John 1:46). "Where did this man get all this?…Is not this the carpenter, the son of Mary?" (Mark 6:2–3).

But to those who did follow him, he gave this answer: "I came from the Father and have come into the world; again, I am leaving the world and am going to the Father." (John 16:28). The uniqueness of Jesus does not rest on his teaching. Jesus is unique because he is the Son of God. This is the claim that Jesus himself made, as the people well recognized. Our faith in Christ as the "Way" to the Father allows us to share in the life of the holy Trinity.

Jesus is the Truth

What do we mean when we say that Jesus "reveals" God to us? Do we mean that, because Jesus comes from God, he can give us inside information that we could not otherwise get? Jesus says of himself, "I am the Truth," not "I speak the truth" or "I reveal the truth," but "I am the Truth."

Jesus not only called on people to believe in his message; he called on people to believe in him. And that was something completely new. There had been prophets and teachers in the past with a message to proclaim, but they had not demanded belief in themselves.

In Jesus, God is actually made present to all. For Jesus is the Son of God—sent into the world by his Father. That astounding fact shines through everything Jesus said and did. In every word and action, Jesus reveals God to us. He shows us, in human terms, what God is like.

In Jesus, God is actually made present to all.

Jesus is the Life

We can never forget that the greatest treasure we have—life itself—is a very fragile possession. The Jewish psalmist put it this way: "Truly, no ransom avails for one's life, there is no price one can give to God for it. For the ransom of life is costly, and can never suffice, that one should live on forever and never see the grave" (Psalm 49:8–9).

In the face of death, we are powerless. It was this awareness that intensified the Jewish desire for a savior. They longed for the gift of everlasting life. Right at the very start of his public preaching Jesus said: "I came that they may have life and have it abundantly" (John 10:10). And as time went on he began to explain to his followers that the life that matters is life everlasting.

HOW We Live It

- *Based on what you think about and do, what would you say is the center of your life?*

- *How has Jesus been the Way in your life? The Truth? The Life?*

- *Which of the Gospel passages cited in this section shows Jesus most clearly for you?*

Saying "Yes" to Jesus

Christ has called each one of us to follow him. How do we respond?

Jesus invited many to become his disciples, to tread the Way of the Cross with him and carry on his mission after him. As the Gospels tell us, some responded enthusiastically: former disciples of John the Baptist, Galilean fishermen, tax collectors—people of all backgrounds and walks of life—accepted his call to follow him.

Not all, however, decided to say yes to Jesus. The Gospels record several incidents in which potential disciples refused to commit themselves to Christ and, therefore, let the opportunity of a lifetime slip away. What choices made the difference between "would-be" disciple and "I-will" disciple?

"I will, but first…"

The Gospels of Matthew and Luke both describe Jesus' encounter with the potential disciples who say they desire to follow Jesus but not quite yet. "Lord, first let me go and bury my father" (Matthew 8:21). "I will follow you, Lord; but let me first say farewell to those at my home" (Luke 9:61).

These people declared their willingness to follow Christ, but at their own convenience; they would accept Christ's invitation on their own terms, not on his. To them, Jesus replied: "Let the dead bury their own dead…No one who puts a hand to the plough and looks back is fit for the kingdom of God" (Luke 9:60, 62).

Those who would accept Jesus' call must do so promptly and enthusiastically, making it their number one priority in life. The Galilean fishermen "left everything and followed him" (Luke 5:11). The tax collector "got up, left everything, and followed him" (Luke 5:28). One's family, career, and personal relationships take on their true meaning only when following Christ is of the utmost importance in life.

"This is a hard saying"

What do you do when you come across something Jesus says that makes you uncomfortable? In the sixth chapter of his Gospel, John gives us the "Bread of Life" discourse, in which Jesus foreshadows his institution of the sacrament of the Eucharist: "Those who eat my flesh and drink my blood have eternal life…; for my flesh is true food and my blood is true drink" (John 6:54–55).

The initial reaction of some of his disciples was shock: "This teaching is difficult; who can accept it?" (v. 60). When Jesus refused to modify his claims, "many of his disciples turned back and no longer went about with him" (v. 66). As long as Jesus' teaching matched their expectations, they were content to follow. When Jesus challenged their presuppositions and declined to tell them simply what they wanted to hear, they parted from him. Their inflexibility and lack of faith proved stronger than their initial commitment to him.

By contrast, when Jesus asked the Twelve, "Do you also wish to go away?" Simon Peter spoke up: "Lord, to whom can we go? You have the words of eternal life. We have come to believe and know that you are the Holy One of God" (vv. 67–69). The faith of the Twelve enabled them to maintain and even strengthen their acceptance of Christ while others retreated, scandalized and confused.

"He went away sad…"

Of all Jesus' encounters with would-be disciples, perhaps the most poignant is his conversation with the rich young man who asked, "'What must I do to inherit eternal life?'… Jesus, looking at him, loved him and said, 'Go, sell what you own, and give the money to the poor, and you will have treasure in heaven; then come, follow me.' When he heard this, he was shocked and went away grieving, for he had many possessions" (Mark 10:17–22).

Although the young man had observed all the commandments of the law, his first allegiance was to his wealth. It would take a profound leap of faith for him to recognize that one's true identity, one's genuine security, can only come from within oneself, from one's internal commitment to Christ. The youth was unable to take that chance, to make that leap of faith in Jesus. He could not be sure that what he would find in Christ, and within himself, would compensate for the surrender of his possessions. So, he left saddened; but he left nonetheless.

"I tell you, I do not know him…"

Probably the saddest loss for Jesus came when, after his arrest, his closest friends ran away. Peter, who had sworn he would die with Jesus, denied Jesus three times.

The disciples had looked forward to power and fame if they stayed with Jesus. He was the Messiah, after all, and to them that meant he would lead Israel to glory. They weren't prepared for the truth, the truth that brought the cross.

None of the Twelve, except John, attended Jesus' crucifixion or burial. Just when Jesus needed them the most, they ran away and locked themselves in a room.

Jesus must have felt sad as he watched all the would-be disciples turn and leave him. Out of fear, insecurity, false pride, arrogance, complacency—as many different motives as there were people—potential disciples hesitated, wavered, teetering on the edge of "yes," but finally refused to follow the only one who could make them truly happy and fulfilled, who could give lasting purpose and direction to their lives.

In truth, there is probably a little bit of the would-be-disciple in each of us—a part of ourselves where we experience doubt, discouragement, or confusion in our relationship to God, family, or Church. There are times when we are tempted to seek our security elsewhere than in Christ and in his love for us; occasions when the demands of discipleship seem too restricting, inconvenient, uncomfortable, or unreasonable.

When we realize we have hesitated and want to turn back, it's time to remember all the disciples who ran away and then returned. Like Peter, we can turn from "I do not know him" to "Lord, you know that I love you." But we must then accept the cost of that discipleship as Peter did.

It is very difficult to give an unconditional "yes" to Christ to embrace wholeheartedly the cross that he asks us to carry with him. But if we ask the Lord to help us make that leap of faith, to remove from our hearts the pride, insecurity, selfishness, or apathy that can cripple discipleship, then we will respond yes ever more generously to him, and need never wonder, with sadness or regret, what might have been.

HOW We Live It

- *Review the events you expect to happen in your life tomorrow: decisions to be made, activities to be enjoyed, people to talk with, and so forth. Choose one of these occasions and examine it. How is it important to you? How is it important to the kingdom of God?*

- *Do we run from the cross? Do we turn our backs on suffering all around us and lock ourselves in our own ignorance?*

Mary

In the Bible, there is one woman described this way: "Blessed are you among women, and blessed is the fruit of your womb" (Luke 1:42).

Catholics throughout the ages have treasured the truth of these words of Elizabeth to Mary. At the center of Catholic faith is Jesus Christ, who is the blessed fruit of the womb of Mary. Close to Jesus, and inseparable from him, is Mary, his mother.

Elizabeth calls her Mother of the Lord (Luke 1:43). God's beautiful plan of redemption called upon the faith, hope, and love of Mary. She said yes: "Let it be with me according to your word" (Luke 1:38). Because she said "yes," Christ was born and we were redeemed.

So, it makes sense that those who confess Jesus Christ as their Lord and Savior will also show honor and respect to his mother, Mary.

God the Father honors Mary. The angel Gabriel, sent from God, announces: "Greetings, favored one! The Lord is with you" (Luke 1:28). God honors Mary by choosing her and allowing the fullness of divinity to take human form in Mary.

Jesus Christ, the Son of God, honors Mary. He chose her to be his mother. At the very beginning of his public life he changes water into wine at the marriage feast at Cana because his mother requests it. (See John 2:1–11.)

The first disciples honored her. She prayed with them while they waited for the coming of the Spirit. (See Acts 1:14.) Just as Jesus is born in Bethlehem of Mary, so the Church of Jesus Christ is born at Pentecost with Mary present.

The early Christian Church honored Mary, and she became a figure for popular devotion among the first Christian communities. As early as AD 150 in the catacombs of Rome, people painted pictures of Mary holding the baby Jesus.

Of course the ultimate reason for honoring Mary is love. If we love Jesus Christ and believe him to be our Lord and Savior, we love Mary, his mother, because she gave him life and nurtured and cared for him until his public ministry began.

As we show respect for our ancestors and other public figures by erecting buildings in their name and fashioning statues in their likeness, so we name churches in Mary's honor and display statues and pictures of Mary, our beloved mother. In doing this, we do not adore or worship Mary: God alone is the object of worship. Mary is a child of God, a creature, and a servant of God.

We consider Mary to be a powerful intercessor with God because of her closeness to God. We, therefore, invoke or call upon Mary to pray to God for us. By calling upon Mary, we share in her holiness and have someone praying for us who is close to Jesus.

Catholics believe that all power, all love, all healing, all graces come from God alone. Thus, we pray in the Hail Mary, "Holy Mary, Mother of God, pray for us sinners, now and at the hour of our death." We simply ask that Mary present our prayers, our needs, to God. In praising Mary, we are praising and thanking God for the power and love God shows to Mary.

Among the different ways of honoring Mary is the praying of the rosary, a centuries-old form of devotion. We also honor Mary by invoking her intercession, but we honor her even more by imitating her virtues. Pope Paul VI encourages this in the following words:

She is held up as an example to the faithful in the way in which, in her own particular life, she fully and responsibly accepted the will of God, because she heard the word of God and acted upon it, and because charity and a spirit of service were the driving force of her actions. She is worthy of imitation because she was the first and the most perfect of Christ's disciples. (On Devotion to the Blessed Virgin Mary, #35).

We call Mary the Mother of God because she is the Mother of Jesus, who is God. As Vatican II puts it: "At the message of the angel, the Virgin Mary received the Word of God in her heart and in her body, and gave life to the world. Hence, she is acknowledged and honored as being truly the Mother of God and Mother of the Redeemer" (Dogmatic Constitution on the Church, #53).

This does not mean that Mary was the source of the divine nature of Jesus, but that she was the mother of his human nature and that there was no time when the human Jesus was not God. The second person of the

Trinity existed for all eternity, but when the "Word became flesh," Jesus was both human and divine from the first moment of his conception. Mary was not the mother of a human being who was adopted as God's son. She was Mother of Jesus Christ, both God and a human. Therefore, it is proper for us to call Mary the "Mother of God."

Another important Catholic truth about Mary is that she is given to us as a mother. "Woman, here is your son," said Jesus on the cross to Mary. "Then he said to the disciple, 'Here is your mother' (John 19:26–27). Most commentators say that the disciple stands for all Christian disciples and that Mary is being presented as mother to all Christian disciples. This led the Church to see and call Mary "Mother of the Church."

What is more, Mary continues this persevering prayer with and for the Church. Taken up into heaven, she did not put aside her saving office of concern for us whom Christ gave to her as her children.

Pope Paul VI said, "Mary, while completely devoted to the will of God, was far from being a timidly submissive woman; on the contrary, she was a woman who did not hesitate to proclaim that God vindicates the humble and the oppressed...She was a woman of strength who experienced poverty and suffering, flight and exile...

and her action helped to strengthen the apostolic community's faith in Christ."

These are all qualities that are just as necessary today as they were in Mary's time.

In praise of all that God had done for her, Mary prayed in her Magnificat (Luke 1:46–55): "Surely, from now on all generations will call me blessed." We are proud to be numbered among the generations that call Mary blessed.

HOW We Live It

- *Look up a few of these Scripture passages about Mary: Luke 1:26–38 (The Annunciation); Luke 1:39–56 (The Visitation); Luke 2:1–21 (The Birth of Jesus); John 2:1–12 (Wedding at Cana); and John 19:25–27 (Standing by the Cross). What one quality of Mary do you admire in these passages?*

- *How could you imitate one of Mary's qualities in your life?*

- *What do you think life was like for Mary, given what we know about her story, her background, her culture, and her environment?*

The Saints

The word used in the Russian Orthodox Church for a saint, "prepodobnia," means "very, very like" and is a perfect description of what Jesus meant by the "true life." If we want to obtain life everlasting, we must become "very, very like" Jesus himself.

The saints are people who lived very much like Jesus did. They are real people who led holy lives that we can use as role models. By honoring saints, the Church makes sure that everyone can benefit from the grace God has worked through holy people.

Saints are not hermits who withdraw from the world. They are not people who never make mistakes or fail or get angry. Saints like to have fun and laugh. Their joy comes from their love of God and their faith that God loved them.

The reason these people are saints is that they faced their mistakes, their struggles, and their joys with a deep love of God and a desire to do God's will completely, no matter what the sacrifice.

Honoring saints was part of Christianity from the very beginning. As a matter of fact, this practice came from a long-standing tradition in the Jewish faith of honoring prophets and holy people with shrines. The first saints were martyrs, people who had given up their lives for the faith because of the persecution of Christians.

At first, saints were recognized by popular acclaim. This was very democratic, but it led to problems. Some people honored saints who were only legends or made up stories about saints. So, by the tenth century, the bishops and the pope took over the authority for approving saints. The procedure the Church uses to name a saint is called canonization.

The canonization process begins after the death of a Catholic who has been considered holy. To be canonized, the candidate's life is examined for heroic virtue or martyrdom, orthodoxy of doctrine, and reputation for holiness. In addition, there needs to be evidence of miracles that have taken place after the candidate's death

The best news about saints is that everyone, including you, is called to be a saint.

as a result of a specific request to the saint for help. These miracles are considered proof that the person is in heaven and can intercede for us.

The title of saint tells us that the person lived a holy life, is in heaven, and is to be honored by the universal Church. But it is important to remember that canonization does not "make" a person a saint. It only recognizes what God has already done. Canonization is also a lengthy, difficult process. So, while every canonized saint is holy, not every holy person has been canonized.

Since saints led holy lives and are close to God in heaven, we feel that their prayers are particularly effective. Often we ask particular saints to pray for us if we feel they have a particular interest in our problem. For example, many people ask Saint Monica to pray for them if they have trouble with unanswered prayers because Monica prayed for twenty years for her son, Augustine, to be converted.

The best news about saints is that everyone, including you, is called to be a saint. Maybe you don't think of yourself as a saint because you have not done anything great. That's no excuse. The saint whom Pope Pius XI called the greatest saint was Thérèse of Lisieux, a Carmelite nun who lived in a cloister and died at 24. What made people all over the world admire her is precisely that she did nothing the world called important but found holiness in everyday things.

There are saints who were twelve years old and saints who lived one hundred years. There are saints and beatified persons from all ethnic and racial backgrounds like Martin de Porres, Kateri Tekakwitha, Juan Diego, and Paul Miki.

There are saints with disabilities, like Julie Billiart, who, though unable to walk for twenty years, taught, organized boycotts, and hid priests during a persecution. There are saints who grew up homeless, like John of the Cross, and saints who grew up to be queens, like Elizabeth of Hungary.

For every excuse you can imagine, God has made a saint who conquered that obstacle. The only thing that can keep you from being a saint is your desire. Do you want to do God's will? Do you want to be transformed by God?

Dorothy Day, cofounder of the Catholic Worker Movement, said: "We are all called to be saints. God expects something from each of us that no one else can do. If we don't, it will not be done."

HOW We Live It

- *Describe someone you know whom you would consider to be "holy." How has this person affected your life?*

- *Have you ever asked anyone to pray for you when you were having a hard time? If so, why did you choose that person?*

- *Are you open to being a saint?*

Conclude the session with
Mary's song of praise from Luke 1:46–51

Mary said, "My soul magnifies the Lord,
and my spirit rejoices in God my Savior,
for he has looked with favor
on the lowliness of his servant.
Surely, from now on all generations
will call me blessed;
for the Mighty One has done
great things for me, and holy is his name.
His mercy is for those who fear him
from generation to generation.
He has shown strength with his arm;
he has scattered the proud
in the thoughts of their hearts."

SUGGESTED RESOURCES

Bauer, Judy and Victoria Hebert. *Wit and Wisdom of the Saints: A Year of Saintly Humor.*

Gittins, Anthony J. *Encountering Jesus: How People Come to Faith and Discover Discipleship.*

Gresham, John L. *Jesus 101: God and Man.*

Zimmer, Mary Ann. *Mary 101: Tradition and Influence.*

Concluding Prayer: O God, we thank you for the gift of Church. Help us see ourselves as valuable members of the body of Christ, each with unique gifts and talents that we bring to the community of faith. Open our eyes to the beauty of your work in all people and in all places, and grant us the grace to grow in faith and love. Amen.

Notes

SESSION 6

The Sacraments: Part One

WHO do we receive in holy Communion and how does it affect us?

WHAT is a sacrament?

WHERE does the tradition of the sacrament of confirmation come from?

WHEN was the ancient catechumenate process reestablished for the whole Church?

WHY must Catholics be baptized before they can celebrate any other sacraments?

Opening Song: "Come, O Spirit of the Lord," by Tom Kendzia, or a hymn of your choice

Opening Prayer: God of all creation, you have called us to this community known as the Catholic Church. Bless our work during this session today, that we may come to better understand who we are and where we come from as members of this Church. Open our minds and our hearts to your word, and to the words of those gathered here with us today. Inspire us with your spirit, and guide us in the way of Jesus, the Christ. Amen.

Reading: John 15:12–17

Spend a moment in quiet reflection.

What Is a Sacrament?

We all know that love is something real. We can experience it, but it's not a physical object. You can't hand someone a piece of love. Love can be conveyed through physical expressions of love, like a hug or a gift of flowers or a favor done for someone dear. These words, gestures, and physical objects become signs of love.

Jesus uses physical signs to communicate his love in the signs of love we call the sacraments. The sacraments are the saving actions of Christ, functioning in the here and now. The physical appearance of Christ is no longer with us, but his words and gestures remain. And because they are the words and gestures of the Spirit-filled body of Christ—the Church—they retain the power of Christ.

There are seven sacraments: baptism, confirmation, Eucharist, reconciliation, holy orders, matrimony, and anointing of the sick.

In the broadest sense, any person, event, or thing through which you encounter God or experience God's presence in a new or deeper way could be called a kind of sacrament. Not only does this perspective heighten our awareness of God's presence in our everyday lives but, paradoxically, it also puts the narrower definition in a new light.

Suddenly, we see things in the seven official sacraments that we hadn't noticed before. For example, it may make us think about how these sacraments originated.

Sacraments started with a human experience of the people who were followers of Jesus. In their contact with the person of Christ, they encountered God in a new way. According to the broad definition, that makes Jesus himself a sacrament, in fact, the sacrament for his disciples. It was through him and him alone that they came to know the Father (see John 8:19; 14:6–10).

In doing that, the early Christians acted just like their ancestors, the Hebrew people. For example, the events of the Exodus story showed the Israelites that God was indeed intimately concerned with their welfare. So the generations to come wouldn't forget, the ancient stories were told and retold, always in the same pattern. These stories, with their standardized words, rich symbols, and interpretative actions, became a cherished ritual—the Passover feast.

For devout Jews (including Jesus) it meant that they also, like their ancestors, were experiencing God's saving power here and now. They were being offered freedom from whatever might be enslaving them and were being invited, right now, to enter into God's kingdom.

When the disciples told their extraordinary story, they used not only words and narratives but also symbolic actions. In other words, they developed significant rituals. For example, the early Christians recalled how Jesus had frequently invited one and all to come and eat with him. We know this loving table-fellowship reached its peak with that very special meal called the Last Supper.

> *The sacraments are the saving actions of Christ, functioning in the here and now.*

Could the disciples forget any of this? Hardly, especially after Jesus had told them to remember it. So, we find them also "breaking bread" and sharing it with others.

In this and other ways, they continued what Jesus had done. They prayed and laid hands on one another, healed, and forgave just as they had seen Jesus pray and lay hands on, heal, and forgive. As Jesus had been the sacrament of God for them, they, the members of his Church, were in turn becoming the sacrament of Jesus for others.

Just as at one time Jesus had used his physical body to carry out the Father's mission, so now he would use the human members of his Church as instruments of salvation. In this way, the risen Lord would be able to do this in an especially direct and tangible way through those seven specialized rituals: the sacraments of the Catholic Church.

The sacraments function like other symbols. That is, they effect, or bring about, what they symbolize. For example, the ritual of baptism symbolizes the soul being cleansed of the "stain" of original sin at the same time that God is making that cleansing happen.

The Church's sacraments grew out of real live experiences; they continue because of an ongoing relationship. Nor was there evidence of nostalgia in the way the disciples thought about Christ. Why should there be? Their faith told them their Lord wasn't really gone: he was still with them in his Spirit.

It's clear that understanding the symbols is essential. The sacraments are Christ's loving gift of himself to his Church; it's folly to ignore them. It's like a starving person who refuses to eat at a banquet.

Think about your human relationships, how they give meaning to your life and are the source of so much happiness. Now, who can say what an encounter with Jesus himself might mean?

Signs of love keep a relationship going. Participating and responding to Jesus' signs of love, the sacraments, keep our encounter with God alive.

HOW We Live It

- *What are some ways that you show the people in your life that you love and care for them?*

- *What are some ways God's love has been revealed to you?*

- *How can you respond to the sacraments in a way that will keep these signs of God's love renewed in your heart?*

The Sacrament of Baptism

The word baptism means a "plunging." In the case of the sacrament of baptism, it is a plunging into the death and resurrection of Christ.

Jesus called his death and resurrection a baptism: "I have a baptism with which to be baptized, and what stress I am under until it is completed" (Luke 12:50).

Here is the double action of our redemption: Christ going down into the grave for our sins and rising again, glorious, triumphant, immortal. But how can we benefit from his gift? We must somehow make personal contact with Christ. We must reach out and become united with his saving death and life-giving resurrection. And we do all of this in baptism.

The Apostle Paul, in his letter to the Romans, puts it this way: "Therefore we have been buried with him by baptism into death, so that, just as Christ was raised from the dead by the glory of the Father, so we too might walk in newness of life" (Romans 6:4).

Saint Paul goes on: "We know that Christ, being raised from the dead, will never die again; death no longer has dominion over him. The death he died, he died to sin, once for all; but the life he lives, he lives to God. So you also must consider yourselves dead to sin and alive to God in Christ Jesus" (Romans 6:9–11).

For Christians, community has always been an essential part of life. Christians form a community in Christ. He is at the center, and the community is built around him.

Baptism is the way we enter that community. We become members of the body of Christ through baptism. We begin to share in the privileges and in the life of this community of believers.

Because baptism confers the character of Christ, it gives the baptized person a share in Christ's priesthood and the power to worship. We must, therefore, be baptized before we can celebrate any other sacraments.

In the years following the death of Jesus, the Church

> *We become members of the body of Christ through the sacrament of baptism.*

established the catechumenate, an extended period of preparation (sometimes lasting three or more years before baptism) to make sure candidates were sincere and well-grounded in the faith. But over the years, as the number of people coming into the Church began to grow, the preparation time began to get shorter and shorter.

By the time Rome fell, baptism was compressed into a brief ritual for infants, symbolizing chiefly the washing away of original sin. This abbreviated ritual eventually was used by missionaries in converting adults, and sometimes hundreds were baptized with little or no preparation.

Until recently, adults who were interested in joining the Catholic Church received private instruction from a priest.

After World War II, the African church began to feel a need for more preparation for its new members and revived the ancient catechumenate process.

Its results were so good that in 1972, the Rite of Christian Initiation of Adults reestablished the ancient catechumenate process for the whole Church. Now, those who are interested in joining the Catholic Church are prepared for the radical step of following Christ and are integrated into the life of the Church through sharing with the community.

Water is the primary symbol of the sacrament of baptism. We know the importance of water for life. We know, too, that a person can live for weeks without food, but for only a few days without water to drink. Scientists believe that all life can be traced to the waters of the sea. They tell us, too, that water is the main element that makes up living tissue—as much as 99 percent. No wonder our Lord chose water to represent the beginning of the new, Christian life. But water reminds us of death as well: tragedies at sea and floods. This is another reason why our Lord chose water to represent the end of the old life and the beginning of the new, Christian life.

God has often used signs of water throughout the Bible. God's Spirit breathed on the waters at the beginning of creation. God parted the Red Sea to lead the Israelites out of slavery into the Promised Land. Naaman was cleansed of leprosy by washing in the Jordan. Water and blood flowed from the side of Christ on the cross.

The waters of baptism remind us that Christ has washed us clean of sin and reconciled us with God. In baptism, all our sins—even original sin—are washed away. That is why the baptismal promises include renunciation of sin and a profession of your personal faith.

If baptism is celebrated separate from confirmation, the newly baptized is anointed with oil. This is a sign that God "has anointed us, by putting his seal on us and giving us his Spirit in our hearts as a first installment" (2 Corinthians 1:21–22). It is a sign that the baptized person shares in the kingly and priestly power of Christ.

Godparents or sponsors place white garments on the newly baptized to show that they have become new creations and have clothed themselves in Christ.

Then, godparents or sponsors light a candle from the Easter candle and present it to the newly baptized. This symbolizes that Christ, the light of the world, is their light, too. And as Paul says, they must "live as children of light" (Ephesians 5:8).

The Church considers Jesus' invitation to baptism to be an invitation of universal and limitless love, an invitation that applies to children as well as to adults.

The Rite of Baptism for Children states: "To fulfill the true meaning of the sacrament, children must later be formed in the faith in which they have been baptized… so that they may ultimately accept for themselves the faith in which they have been baptized."

A person enters "into Christ" at the time of baptism. That means the gift of the Spirit also is given at that time. "For all who are led by the Spirit of God are children of God....It is that very Spirit bearing witness with our spirit that we are children of God, and if children, then heirs, heirs of God and joint heirs with Christ" (Romans 8:14–17).

As adopted sons and daughters of God, Christians share in Jesus' own relationship with his Father—a relationship so intimate that they, like Jesus, can freely and with every confidence address the Lord of heaven as "Father."

The person who is plunged into the baptismal font emerges from the waters a new creature with a new life. This new life is the Holy Spirit, who makes a home in us and gives us the power not only to know God but also to do all that God requires.

HOW We Live It

- *Name one part of your life that would change if you died to sin and lived for God.*

- *What would a new life "in Christ" be for you?*

- *As a child and heir of God, what riches do you inherit? What responsibilities?*

The Sacrament of the Eucharist

The Catholic Church teaches that the Eucharist is both a meal and a sacrifice.

During the Last Supper, with his closest friends and followers, Jesus spelled out—by word, "This is my body....This is my blood," and action, the breaking of the bread—how the Father's forgiveness and the New Covenant would come about.

This meal held a powerful message for the disciples: If they truly heeded his words and actions, if they lived up to what this meal required of them, they, like Jesus, should be ready, if necessary, to lay down their lives for others.

In studies of the Jewish culture of Jesus' time, there are indications that Jesus' words alone would not have been enough for his enemies to first issue a death sentence and, second, hand over a fellow Jew to the hated Roman authorities. What was the great crime that this maverick rabbi from Galilee had committed?

Recent research has come up with this: What scandalized and infuriated the Jewish leaders was that Jesus frequently and deliberately sat down and ate meals with outcasts. That means he ate not only with his regular followers, mostly uneducated Galilean fishermen but, much worse, he insisted on welcoming even the despised "tax collectors and sinners."

Scholar Norman Perrin remarks: "It is hard to imagine anything more offensive to Jewish sensibilities. To have become such an outcast himself would have been much less of an outrage than to welcome those people back into the community....The central feature of the message of Jesus is, then the challenge of the forgiveness of sins and the offer of the possibility of a new kind of relationship with God and with one's fellow [human]. This was symbolized by a table-fellowship which celebrated the present joy and anticipated the future consummation."

Now, we must try to understand the meaning of sacrifice—a notion sometimes foreign to our culture and practice—in biblical times. Let's imagine a Jewish family coming to the temple to offer sacrifice. They don't bring gold but something connected with life, such as a living animal or fruits of the harvest.

They make their way to the sanctuary, where there is an altar. But the harvesting of the wheat or the slaying of the dove or lamb is not a gesture of sacrifice. The sacrifice occurs when the priest puts the fruits or blood on the altar and the people make an internal offering of themselves. They struggle to offer their very lives in the service of the Lord.

When we receive holy Communion, we receive the whole person of Christ.

The Christian community has always acknowledged that Jesus' death on the cross was the greatest of all sacrifices. Again, this is so because of what went on in his mind and heart. He really made an offering of himself—a free, sacrificial offering.

Catholics believe that when Jesus said, "This is my body....This is my blood," he meant exactly what he said. For Jews, body meant the person, and blood was the source of life identifiable with the person. So Jesus was saying over the bread and cup, "This is myself," and we believe that the consecrated bread and wine truly become the very person of Jesus.

The New Testament bears witness to the reality of Christ's presence in the Eucharist. The sixth chapter of John's Gospel is devoted to Jesus as the "Bread of Life." Jesus tells us: "I am the living bread that came down from heaven....Very truly, I tell you, unless you eat the flesh of the Son of Man and drink his blood, you have no life in you. Those who eat my flesh and drink my blood have eternal life, and I will raise them up on the last day" (John 6:51–54).

Many disciples found these words intolerable and left Jesus. But Jesus did not say, "Wait, I meant that the bread only represents my body." Instead, he asked the Twelve, "Do you also wish to go away?" Peter answered him, "Lord, to whom can we go? You have the words of eternal life" (John 6:67–68).

Like Peter, Catholics do not claim to understand how bread and wine become Christ's body and blood. We accept, as Peter did, the "words of eternal life" on the authority of Jesus. Since the twelfth century, the Church has used the word "transubstantiation" to describe the change from the "substance" of bread to the "substance" of the flesh of Christ. To express the original meaning of substance, we need to speak about the inner reality of a thing, the deepest level of its being.

The "appearances"—the outer characteristics like taste, color, and weight of the bread and wine—remain just as they were before the consecration, but the deep realities have been changed into the body and blood of the living Christ. When we receive holy Communion, then we receive the whole person of Christ, as he is at the present moment, that is, as risen Lord, with his glorified body and soul, and his full divinity.

Jesus always invited everyone who would come share a meal with him. This is what the community is called to do every time it gathers around the altar. In this way, it becomes the sacrament of the resurrected Savior. And when that happens, people can discover an experiential point of departure for affirming their faith. Now the people can experience this presence of their Lord and master both in the consecrated species and in the community gathered around the table.

As Saint Augustine put it: "We must be what we have eaten." We are already the body of Christ but we must become that body still more. We must be bread for others just as Jesus is bread given for us—bread, broken and shared, as nourishment for our brothers and sisters in Christ. We are God's people only insofar as we are willing to become bread and wine, nourishment and life, body and blood for all other human beings.

HOW We Live It

- *With whom have you associated who has caused people to talk?*

- *Is there someone you would refuse to eat with or keep company with? How can you act like Jesus toward this person?*

- *What does sacrifice mean to you? How does Jesus' sacrifice on the cross impact your life, and your appreciation of the Eucharist?*

The Sacrament of Confirmation

Jesus promised the apostles that he would give them the courage they needed to face any fears about serving him (Acts 1:8). It was a promise he kept.

"When the day of Pentecost had come, they were all together in one place. And suddenly from heaven there came a sound like the rush of a violent wind, and it filled the entire house where they were sitting. Divided tongues, as of fire, appeared among them, and a tongue rested on each of them. All of them were filled with the Holy Spirit and began to speak in other languages, as the Spirit gave them ability" (Acts 2:1–4).

Confirmation confers the courage and gifts of the Holy Spirit that we need to be witnesses to Christ in our daily lives. Christ is still fulfilling his promise through the sacrament of confirmation.

Because of the close connection between baptism and confirmation, the early Christians normally conferred them together in one rite. In the New Testament, nonetheless, the foundation for the clear distinction between them is evident. For example, Philip the deacon sent for the Apostles Peter and John to "come and lay hands" on some women and men whom he had baptized "and they received the Holy Spirit" (Acts 8:14–17).

After Paul baptized some disciples of John the Baptist, he also laid hands on them and then "the Holy Spirit came upon them, and they spoke in tongues and prophesied" (Acts 19:1–7). The Letter to the Hebrews speaks of "baptisms" and "laying on of hands" as two distinct actions (Hebrews 6:2).

The truth, of course, is that the Holy Spirit is given in both baptism and confirmation. But the function of the Holy Spirit in each is different. The difference is hinted at by Saint Augustine when he explains that in baptism we are mixed with water so that we might take on the form of bread, the body of Christ. But bread, he points out, then needs to be baked in the fire; and this fire is supplied by the chrism which is "the sacrament of the Holy Spirit," who was revealed in tongues of fire.

At baptism, in other words, we are made members of Christ's body. But at confirmation we are given the power of God to bear fruit in our Christian life and to speak before the world boldly, and so draw others into the Church.

Christ has shown us the way to spiritual maturity. He has given us the Holy Spirit, who gives us the strength to face up to our responsibilities and to share the Gospel with others. The Holy Spirit helps us grow in our faith and in our discipleship; this is the meaning of the sacrament of confirmation.

Maturity always brings with it a greater sensitivity and responsibility toward those around us. And that is why the sacrament of confirmation is often referred to as the sacrament of social action. The strengthening and increased maturity we receive in this sacrament are not only for our own benefit. They are given to us by the Holy Spirit so we can contribute actively and creatively to the family life of the Church and the world.

We all have our own special gifts and talents. And in one way or another, we have many opportunities to help the Church in the world.

The sacrament of confirmation is conferred by the laying on of hands followed by the anointing with chrism on the forehead in the form of a cross.

The laying on of hands is an important biblical gesture by which the Holy Spirit is asked to come to you. In the Gospels, Jesus healed many people with a touch. When the woman with a hemorrhage touched his cloak with faith she would be healed, he said he experienced power going out from him.

The anointing is done with chrism, olive oil mixed with balsam. The oil is a symbol of strength; the perfume is a symbol of the "fragrance of Christ," which the Christian must spread. The chrism must have been consecrated by the bishop. The word "Messiah" and "Christ" both mean "anointed one." The Israelites anointed priests, and later kings, as a sign that they were chosen by God. Like these priests and kings, you are chosen by God. And like them, you are being anointed or chosen for a purpose.

Older Catholics may remember the "slap on the

Confirmation confers the courage and gifts of the Holy Spirit that we need to be witnesses to Christ.

cheek" that used to be part of the rite of confirmation. However, like many other little ceremonies in the Church's liturgy, this disappeared in 1971 when the new rite of confirmation was promulgated. Today, the bishop says simply, "Peace be with you;" and the new confirmand replies, "And also with you."

It is normally the bishop, the leader of the community, who administers the sacrament (although a priest may do so under certain circumstances), symbolizing that confirmation is a "confirming" of the Christian's initiation into the community.

In confirmation, the sponsor places a hand on the candidate's shoulder as a sign that the sponsor is presenting the candidate for confirmation on behalf of the whole Christian community. Each sponsor undertakes to encourage the confirmed Christian to fulfill the promise to be Christ's witness.

The word "sponsor" comes from the same root as "responsible," a root that means "someone who guarantees, pledges, promises." A sponsor needs to be a person who can travel with you on your journey to Christian maturity. This person should know you and be readily available to listen to your concerns and questions about your faith or about the Church. Choices for sponsors might include parishioners you admire and see quite often.

Whomever you choose, your sponsor must be sufficiently mature, belong to the Catholic Church, and be initiated into the three sacraments of baptism, confirmation, and the Eucharist. The most important thing though, is that you and your sponsor will have more than an acquaintance-type relationship. Your sponsor needs to be a spiritual friend to you.

In confirmation, Christians are "anointed" with the power of the Holy Spirit to profess their faith within the Church and to testify to the truth to those outside it. Therefore, the Catholic Church believes that it would be more beneficial for those older who are able to witness.

We should always remember, however, that the Christian life in all its aspects is the first gift of the Spirit. Moreover, each person has special gifts that the Holy Spirit uses for the good of the whole Church.

Always remember to ask the Spirit to help you reach for these gifts when you need them. And remember these words of Saint Cyril of Jerusalem: "Please be aware of how great a dignity Jesus bestows on you.... The indwelling Spirit makes your mind a house of God."

HOW We Live It

- *What "childish ways" do you have to put away to grow as a Christian?*

- *Look up Isaiah 11:2–3, and reflect on the gifts of the Spirit. Which of these gifts do you need most in your life right now? Why?*

- *How does the Holy Spirit help you witness to your faith?*

Conclude the session by reading this excerpt from the Prayer to the Holy Spirit:

*O God, you have instructed the hearts
of the faithful
by the light of the Holy Spirit.
Grant that through the same Holy Spirit we may
always be truly wise and rejoice in the
Spirit's consolation.
Through Christ our Lord. Amen.*

SUGGESTED RESOURCES

Altemose, Charlene. *What You Should Know About the Sacraments.*

Chesto, Kathleen. The "Touched by Grace" series on sacraments.

Redemptorist Fathers. *The Essential Catholic Handbook of the Sacraments: A Summary of Beliefs, Rites, and Prayers.*

Vomund, Jeff. *What Catholics Believe About ...* DVDs on Sacraments, Baptism, Confirmation, and the Eucharist.

Concluding Prayer: O God, we thank you for the gift of Church. Help us see ourselves as valuable members of the body of Christ, each with unique gifts and talents that we bring to the community of faith. Open our eyes to the beauty of your work in all people and in all places, and grant us the grace to grow in faith and love. Amen.

SESSION 7

The Sacraments: Part Two

WHO can receive the sacrament of the anointing of the sick?

WHAT is the purpose of the sacrament of reconciliation/penance?

WHERE can we catch a glimpse of the oneness of God in the sacrament of matrimony?

WHEN did celibacy become mandatory for priests of the Latin Rite of the Roman Catholic Church?

WHY do Catholics confess their sins to a priest?

Opening Song: "Balm in Gilead," or a hymn of your choice

Opening Prayer: God of all creation, you have called us to this community known as the Catholic Church. Bless our work during this session today, that we may come to better understand who we are and where we come from as members of this Church. Open our minds and our hearts to your word, and to the words of those gathered here with us today. Inspire us with your spirit, and guide us in the way of Jesus, the Christ. Amen.

Reading: John 8:1–11

Spend a moment in quiet reflection.

Why Do We Need to Reconcile?

Sin is turning away from God, as well as turning away from ourselves and others. The origination of sin and its effects can be found in the creation story of Genesis. At first, Adam and Eve experienced an inner harmony with self, God, each other, and creation. Then the serpent entered the garden and sin was committed.

God and the Church tell us that certain behaviors are sinful because they are destructive to human and spiritual growth. Our growth as human and spiritual persons is very much dependent on our ability to give and receive love from God and others.

While most people believe that refusing to love others is sinful, not too many are aware that refusing to accept love from God and others is just as sinful—simply because such refusal is destructive to our growth as human and spiritual persons.

So often, when we are hurt or feel bad about ourselves, we withdraw and refuse to love. This means that other people, especially people close to us, are denied a kind of nourishment. Likewise, when we refuse to accept the love that God and others offer us, we shut ourselves off from the wellsprings of life.

A person in sin, especially serious sin, is a person alone and disintegrating. In this state, the human being is a person in need of penance and reconciliation.

Penance, which consists of conversion of heart (contrition), forgiveness of sin (confession), and restoration of relationships (satisfaction), was central to the ministry of Jesus. (See Luke 15:11–24.) His ministry reveals that Jesus didn't come to just reconcile or save souls: Jesus came to reconcile and save persons. Understanding this incarnate aspect of Jesus' ministry is essential for our understanding of the Church and all the sacramental aspects of Christianity.

The apostolic community believed Jesus had given it the power to forgive sins: "He breathed on them and said to them: 'If you forgive the sins of any, they are forgiven them; if you retain the sins of any, they are retained'" (John 20:22–23).

Even though Jesus gave his disciples—the Church—the authority to forgive sins in his name, he did not spell out for them a detailed way to exercise this authority. Perhaps he thought it best to leave to the Church of every age the authority to create meaningful rites through which post-baptismal sin would be forgiven and healed.

The purpose of the sacrament of penance and reconciliation is to help us celebrate and deepen our ongoing efforts to be people of reconciliation in our world.

Therefore, participation in this sacrament assumes that we are making sincere efforts in our daily lives to become more Christlike and are trying to fulfill our call to be ambassadors of reconciliation.

As ambassadors of reconciliation we are called to be God's instruments in removing the barriers that keep individuals and groups from communicating with and caring for each other. Participation in this sacrament also implies that, as God freely forgives us our transgressions, we, too, are willing to freely give and receive forgiveness.

Perhaps too often the sacrament is used as a means to get rid of guilt feelings or to wipe our slate clean. In such situations, the primary focus is on self and not on reconciliation with God and others. Ideally, we ought to participate in the sacrament in response to the prompting of the Holy Spirit calling us to conversion in some specific areas of our lives. If the sacrament is seen in a narrow, individualistic manner and not in the broader context of the call to be reconcilers in a divided world, then it will lose much of its power and meaning.

Confession is psychologically healthy. By naming and confronting our sinful acts and habits they lose much of their power over us. Karl Menninger, a well-known psychiatrist, startled many people when he wrote a book titled, "Whatever Became of Sin?" and said that much psychiatric counseling failed because often it is only an attempt to rationalize sin and wrongdoing. Facing sin and taking responsibility for one's behavior is good "reality therapy," inside or outside the reconciliation room.

The Catholic Church asks its members to confess

> *A person in sin, especially serious sin, is a person alone and disintegrating.*

their sins to a priest because the Church has always believed that sin, however private, is a community affair. When we are baptized we are grafted onto the body of Christ. No part of the human body can suffer pain without all parts being diminished or affected. What is true of the human body is also true of the body of Christ (the Church). When any of its members sin, they all suffer.

Penitents are asked to reflect deeply in preparing themselves for the sacrament. In the examination of conscience, the underlying aim is to get in touch with the general flow or tone of one's spiritual life. The aim is not to come up with a superficial "grocery list" of quickly thought-up sins but to get in touch with attitudes and patterns of behavior that are destructive to one's relationship with God, others, and self.

In the confessional, the priest is the representative of God and the community. In the reconciliation room, the priest represents the whole Christ—the head (Jesus) and the members (the Church).

When we leave the reconciliation room we have been forgiven of the sins we confessed and the sins we unintentionally omitted. The sacrament is like a second baptism and now we make a new beginning.

HOW We Live It

- *How would you define sin?*

- *Where might there be a need for a conversion in your life, for example, from attitudes or behaviors that were keeping you from God?*

- *Is there someone with whom you may need or want to be reconciled at this time? If so, how might you go about doing this?*

The Sacrament of Anointing of the Sick

In ancient times, there was no sharp distinction drawn between one's physical well-being and spiritual well-being. Those suffering a physical ailment suffered mentally and emotionally as well; those depressed or guilt-ridden often showed physical symptoms. There was a holistic attitude about the relationship between soul and body.

Jesus shared this attitude toward health and sickness. He was concerned about the physical health of people, as well as their spiritual health. In fact, the word "salvation" is derived from the Latin *salus*, which means "health." By healing people's bodies as well as their souls, Jesus showed that the entire human being is touched by God's salvation.

Jesus' ministry to people was a healing ministry in both senses of the word. He healed spiritual lives by assuring people that God forgives them their sins and gives them the power to love and care for others. Jesus also healed physical ailments as a sign of God's power and as an example of caring that accounts for the entire person.

James 5:14–15 tells us: "Are any among you sick? They should call for the elders of the church and have them pray over them, anointing them with oil in the name of the Lord. The prayer of faith will save the sick, and the Lord will raise them up; and anyone who has committed sins will be forgiven."

Today, the rite of anointing is celebrated along with a Liturgy of the Word so that those gathered for the sacrament may be instructed on the deeper Christian meaning of sickness and celebrate the sacrament in renewed faith.

This is followed by the laying on of hands, an ancient Christian gesture. In silence, the priest imposes hands on the heads of those to be anointed. In both the Old and New Testaments, the laying on of hands symbolizes and confers the giving of the special grace of the

God's communication to the sick is always real and total.

Holy Spirit. Here the sick are singled out for the Spirit's special care.

Next, the blessing of, or thanksgiving over, the oil is given. As a symbol of the penetrating presence of the Holy Spirit, oil is particularly apt for the anointing of the sick. As the oil is rubbed and absorbed into the skin, so does the Holy Spirit "enter" the sick person, claiming, empowering, enlivening, and rejuvenating in the name of Christ.

The final step in the ritual is the actual anointing, which is done to the head and to the hands. The forehead is anointed because there the sign of the cross was first traced when the candidates for Christian initiation became catechumens, at baptism, and at confirmation.

The rubbing of oil into the hands signifies the Holy Spirit meeting us in our personal situation, in our own particular sickness with its unique set of feelings. Whether we feel pain, resentment, denial, acceptance, or even joy, the anointing oil will bring Christ the healer to us in our special circumstances.

The various prayers after the anointing make it clear that the God-given grace of the sacrament is "tailor-made" to suit the sick person's particular needs. In other words, one can expect God to give exactly what is needed at that moment to assure salvation and to fulfill the Christian vocation.

Whatever the person's particular need and consequent grace, it must be remembered that God's self-communication to the sick is always real and total—not just to the body, not just to the spirit, but to the whole person.

Not long ago anointing of the sick was mostly for those close to death. Calling for a priest to administer "extreme unction," as it was then called, indicated that the doctor did not give the patient long to live.

The Second Vatican Council helped restore this sacrament to its original purpose. They changed the name from extreme unction to anointing of the sick. They also said that it "is not a sacrament intended only for those who are at the point of death. Hence, it is certain that as soon as any of the faithful begins to be in danger of death from sickness or old age, this is already a suitable time for them to receive this sacrament" (The Constitution on the Sacred Liturgy, #73).

This meant that Catholics could be anointed as soon as they learned they had any illness that might lead to death. They could even request the sacrament if they were going to have an operation since sometimes even simple operations lead to complications. The Church also recognized that those advanced in years had a right to be anointed since older persons are closer to death because of the illnesses to which they are susceptible.

The sacraments of reconciliation, anointing of the sick, and Eucharist, administered together for a dying person, are properly called the last rites of the Church. In this situation, prayers associated with the anointing are modified slightly to ask more for spiritual strength rather than physical healing.

Priests are the only ones who can sacramentally anoint the sick. Ministry to the sick, however, is recognized as a concern of the entire Christian community, not just the priest. Many persons experience both spiritual and physical healing when others pray over them and ask God to heal them.

Professional healthcare givers as well as family and friends can do much to meet the spiritual needs of people who are ill. Keep in mind that spiritual needs include the forgiveness of sins, the need to know they will be cared for, that they are loved despite any disabilities or deformities, that they will be supported regardless of the cost, and that they will not be abandoned in their final hours.

Other spiritual needs include the need to come to terms with debilitating physical conditions, to forgive self and others for any carelessness or malice that has led to the injury or condition, to re-establish communication with estranged loved ones, and to be reconciled with God before death.

We are all challenged to do everything we can to reach out to those who are suffering, just as Jesus taught his followers to do, just as Jesus did himself. Christians who do this continue the healing ministry of Jesus and the early Church.

Jesus cared for the total person, body and soul. The kingdom of God that Jesus announced was not something we have to die to enter, but something we can begin to experience today, here and now.

HOW We Live It

- *What are your feelings about the anointing of the sick? Have you ever taken part in this sacrament?*

- *Describe a time when you were healed physically, spiritually, or emotionally. Has there ever been a time when your physical health was affected by your mental health or vice versa?*

- *Do you think sickness can be a blessing? In what way?*

The Sacrament of Marriage

Christian marriage is a personal relationship of life-giving love in which a man and a woman make the love of Christ present to each other and become a sign of the love of Christ to those around them. In marriage, the relationship of the couple reveals the love of God for people.

Jesus showed us God's design for marriage in many ways. He was born into a human family, thereby showing the holiness of ordinary family life (Luke 2). He worked his first miracle at the wedding feast of Cana (John 2:1–11), putting the seal of God's approval on marriage. He taught that married love must be faithful (Matthew 5:27–28), and proclaimed that married love was meant to last forever (Mark 10:6–8).

Marriage is not just the situation in which married people serve God. It is precisely their love for each other that is their service of God, the way in which they make Christ present to each other. That's why the ministers of the sacrament of marriage are the husband and wife themselves.

Founded on God's giving of God's self, married love is based on giving. Total loving means total giving. It is not just a question of "giving up" something.

In marriage, the gift given is oneself. Married love is not just a feeling, but a choice one makes to love the other person unconditionally. In choosing to love, we make the decision to give without resentment, to forgive fully, to put the other's needs before our own. Two people joined in marriage become one as they share freely the unique gifts alive in them for the sake of the other.

God's faithfulness to people is evident in the commitment a couple makes to love each other for a lifetime. That love requires a sacrifice for the good of the other. This is not just in the major things like illness or tragedy. It is listening when the other needs to talk rather than going to sleep; trying to affirm instead of criticize; allowing laughter to end a quarrel instead of insisting on being right. It is sharing hurts and fears instead of hiding them and being independent. It is understanding that some people just can't balance a checkbook; it is disciplining the children together.

God's faithfulness accepts us for who we are, affirms us, looks for the good in us, and helps us grow. A married couple should challenge all of us to an understanding that doesn't give up on others, but looks for the gifts in each one, affirms those gifts, and draws them forth for the good of the community.

Jesus revealed God's original intention for married love. "So they are no longer two, but one flesh. Therefore what God has joined together, let no one separate" (Mark 10:6–9). His words indicate God's presence in the physical as well as spiritual union of husband and wife and point to a special importance of the marital relationship, that is even more sacred than that of parent and child, and cannot be broken by civil divorce.

When their marriage breaks down, some Catholics get a civil divorce in order to protect their safety or security. Catholics believe a marriage between Christians can never be dissolved. So, although for legal reasons a Catholic may get a civil divorce, the Church still considers them to be married and they cannot remarry in the Church without the benefit of an annulment. Catholics also believe a marriage between two Protestants cannot be broken by divorce any more than a marriage between two Catholics can be broken because both marriages are sacramental.

Annulment is not a Catholic divorce, but the official Church recognition that the marriage was not a true marriage in the first place. This can only be if, on examination, it is found that one or more of the requirements of a valid marriage were not present. These requirements are stated in the marriage papers, when the couple is asked to affirm: "I understand the nature and essential obligations of Christian marriage. Accordingly, I am entering marriage freely; I intend to be faithful until death; I pray our marriage will be blessed with offspring."

Investigating an annulment involves a long procedure and requires witnesses and evidence to support

> *Founded on God's giving of God's self, married love is based on giving.*

any claim of invalidity. It cannot be bought or arranged. A decree of nullity in no way affects the legitimacy of any children of the marriage.

God's love is passionate and joyful and intimate, and it is reflected in a couple's passion for each other. The intimacy enjoyed in marriage is sexual, emotional, and spiritual. "Making love" is a good description of intimacy because that is just what it should do. It not only expresses the love of husband and wife but also makes their love for each other grow.

Because they share in God's creative love, a couple is privileged to share in the most exalted part of God's creative work—the creation of another human being. Their generosity and love is surely a brilliant reflection of the Creator's love when God first brought the world into being. An essential dimension of the sacrament of marriage is a willingness to empower one's spouse to be a parent. This is more than the act of conception: it is the encouragement and support given to each other during the raising of the children. This willingness to bring life through each other and to mutually share in the work of nurturing that life to adulthood stands as a challenge to us, the community of believers. Because

couples help each other grow in marriage, creativity is still present in the marriages of those who can't have children.

It is impossible to understand the oneness of God the Father, God the Son, and God the Holy Spirit. But it is possible to recognize the strength and beauty of a couple who is truly one. Each person is distinct, and yet together they are a more complete whole. Each of us reveals the dimensions of God in different ways, yet it is specifically in terms of the relationship that God is best revealed, because God is relationship.

In the blending of the two into one flesh, we, the Church, can catch a glimpse of the oneness of God.

HOW We Live It

- *What does true love mean to you?*

- *Describe an example of faithfulness in marriage. What has it shown you about God's faithfulness to us?*

- *In what ways is God's love for you passionate and intimate?*

The Sacrament of Holy Orders

The sacrament of holy orders establishes bishops, priests, and deacons as legitimate leaders within the community of the Church.

In the Gospels, there is no clearly defined ceremony of ordination for the apostles. In fact, the word "priest" was not applied to the leaders of the new Church for the first hundred years after Christ's ascension.

But there can be no doubt that the apostles served the Church as the first priests and bishops. They were closely connected to the work of Christ while he was on earth. They received special instruction, spent much time with him, and saw the miracles he performed.

Jesus sent the apostles out to preach and baptize (see Matthew 10). They were given the power to heal (see Mark 6:1–3) and to forgive sins (see John 20:23). At the Last Supper, when our Lord instructed the apostles to "do this in memory of me," he was giving them the power to preside at the Eucharist.

In the early Church, it was clear that all baptized believers shared in the universal priesthood of Christ. The early Christians recognized and made use of the different charisms that contributed to the building up of the priestly community. Others could heal, work miracles, or prophesy. Still others could speak in tongues or discern the Spirit.

The leaders were chosen especially to preach and teach. Their office was signified by the imposition of hands and the calling down of the Holy Spirit (see 2 Timothy 1:6–7). Everyone could proclaim the word and witness to the faith, but only the ordained leader had the power to preach in the assembly, to lead the Eucharist, and to guide the community.

As the Church continued to expand, the role of the priest became more important. Often, he was the most well-educated person in the community, and because of this a tendency arose to concentrate ever more roles in this person. Eventually, the priests and bishops became a special class in the Church. The doctrine of universal priesthood gradually fell into abeyance until the Second Vatican Council.

The council noted that the priest's chief responsibilities are to bring about the presence of Christ in the Church and to share in Christ's office as teacher, sanctifier, and leader. He is chosen to act in the person of Christ. He is to preach the Gospel, give pastoral service to the faithful, and celebrate the Mass and the sacraments. His ministerial priesthood is distinct from the priesthood of the faithful "in essence and degree." His powers are conferred through the sacrament of holy orders.

In making this distinction, however, the council pointed out that every effort must be made to actualize the priesthood of all the faithful. All people need to hear the good news and to experience Christ in their lives. This can only come about through the common effort of all persons baptized into the universal priesthood working along with the ordained priests.

In the early Church, it was clear that all baptized believers shared in the universal priesthood of Christ.

Most people think of holy orders in terms of priesthood, but priesthood is really the second level of holy orders. The bishop, at his consecration, receives the fullness of the sacrament. But a deacon also receives this sacrament.

The office of bishop in the Church can be traced back to Christ's commissioning the apostles. The bishops are the successors to the apostles. By the year 110, the bishop served as head of the local Church as the representative of Christ. He was also the one to guarantee the unity of the Church in a specific area and to ensure the harmony of his believers with those throughout the Church.

As the principal teacher in his diocese, the bishop sees that the truths of the Catholic faith and the principles of morality are taught correctly. As first among preachers, he speaks in the name of Christ. He governs the people as the vicar of Christ. In his own diocese, the bishop is clearly the head of the Church.

In the early Church, the bishops ministered to everyone. As the number of believers grew, the bishops were no longer able to care for all Church members. Therefore they ordained men to act in their place, and these men were called priests. From the beginning of the second century, the priest ranked between the deacon and the bishop. He was ordained to function in the name of the bishop. His duties were to preach and sanctify. It was his privilege to lead the people in prayer and at the Eucharist.

The same relationship exists today. When the priest preaches, teaches, or offers the sacrifice of the Mass, he does so in the name of the bishop.

The activities of today's priest fall into three basic categories. First, he is called to preach by word and action. His message should bring people the good news of salvation and lead them to conversion, renewal, and growth. Second, he is the leader of worship. He represents Christ performing the actions of salvation for the community. In doing this, he becomes a sign of Christ's presence among the people. Third, he is to be a leader. Taking the image of the good shepherd, he gives himself to the people of his Church and the world.

The priest can celebrate the sacraments of baptism, the Eucharist, reconciliation, anointing of the sick, and be the official witness at marriages. He can celebrate confirmation in special circumstances with permission of the bishop.

The word "deacon" comes from a Greek word that means "servant" or "helper." The order of deacon receives a lot of attention in the New Testament. The deacons are instructed to assist the apostles as they serve the people. It is quite clear that the deacons are to be strong believers, upright Christians, and men dedicated to the service of the community and the spread of the Gospel (see 1 Timothy 3:8–13).

There are two types of deacons. The transitional diaconate is the step before ordination as a priest. In the permanent diaconate, a man does not make the transition to the priesthood but remains a deacon. With the permission of the bishop, the deacon can baptize, distribute the Eucharist at Mass or Communion services, bring Communion to the sick, and officiate at marriages and funerals. He leads the people in prayer, reads the Scriptures, preaches, and teaches. He serves the people of God working in the image of Christ and following the example of those first deacons in the early Church. A married man may be ordained as a permanent deacon. If a deacon is single or if his wife dies, however, he must remain unmarried.

Celibacy, the voluntary state of not marrying and of abstaining from sexual intercourse, is mentioned in the New Testament, for example, Matthew 19:12 and 1 Corinthians 7:32–34. Some priests in the early Church freely embraced celibacy and, in 1139, celibacy became mandatory for priests of the Latin Rite of the Roman Catholic Church. Married men may be ordained priests in Eastern Rite Catholic Churches, and, today, married ministers of other faiths who join the Roman Catholic Church and are ordained to the priesthood may remain married.

Celibacy frees priests from many concerns, as Saint Paul suggests, to devote themselves to "the things of the Lord." Celibacy is a positive surrender of self to Christ, not just a negative renunciation, just as marriage is the positive choosing of one spouse, not just the renunciation of all others.

In Jesus, God gave us God-made-flesh. And this is what we look for in the priesthood: Christ made present to us in a person.

HOW We Live It

- *Can you think of an example of a leader who serves?*

- *Have you known priests who have contributed to growth in your spiritual life? In what ways?*

**Conclude the session by reading
1 Corinthians 13:1–7:**

*"If I speak in the tongues of mortals and of
angels, but do not have love, I am a noisy gong
or a clanging cymbal. And if I have prophetic
powers, and understand all mysteries and all
knowledge, and if I have all faith, so as to remove
mountains, but do not have love, I am nothing.
If I give away all my possessions,
and if I hand over my body so that I may boast,
but do not have love, I gain nothing.
Love is patient; love is kind;
love is not envious or boastful or arrogant or rude.
It does not insist on its own way;
it is not irritable or resentful;
it does not rejoice in wrongdoing,
but rejoices in the truth. It bears all things,
believes all things, hopes all things,
endures all things."*

SUGGESTED RESOURCES

Dowling, John R. *Why Confess Your Sins to a Priest?*

Gaillardets, Richard R. *A Daring Promise: A Spirituality of
Christian Marriage.*

Mathis, Rick. *Prayer-Centered Healing: Finding the God
Who Heals.*

Redemptorist Fathers. *What Catholics Believe About
Reconciliation* DVD.

Concluding Prayer: O God, we thank you for the gift of Church. Help us see ourselves as valuable members of the body of Christ, each with unique gifts and talents that we bring to the community of faith. Open our eyes to the beauty of your work in all people and in all places, and grant us the grace to grow in faith and love. Amen.

SESSION 8

Christian Living: Part One

WHO can we turn to for moral guidance in today's world?

WHAT is conscience and how is it formed?

WHERE does Jesus urge us to move in his teaching?

WHEN did the Catholic Church begin addressing modern social issues?

WHY should we, as Catholics, be concerned about injustice and social issues?

Opening Song: "We Walk By Faith," by Marty Haugen, or a hymn of your choice

Opening Prayer: God of all creation, you have called us to this community known as the Catholic Church. Bless our work during this session today, that we may come to better understand who we are and where we come from as members of this Church. Open our minds and our hearts to your word, and to the words of those gathered here with us today. Inspire us with your spirit, and guide us in the way of Jesus, the Christ. Amen.

Reading: Matthew 22:37–40

Spend a moment in quiet reflection.

Morality and Conscience

How do we know what is right or wrong? Something is right and moral if it is right in the eyes of God, wrong and immoral if it is wrong in the eyes of God. Saint Paul tells us that some of the most basic notions of right and wrong are written in our hearts by God (see Romans 2:15).

Conscience is our sense of the moral goodness or evil of a thing. My conscience is myself, as I have the ability to discern right or wrong and the responsibility to choose what is right.

How is conscience formed? We begin by responding to the call of Jesus, "Those who love me will keep my word, and my Father will love them, and we will come to them and make our home with them" (John 14:23). We accept Jesus Christ as our guide, believing that his words and example teach us the best way to live. We study his teachings and try to apply them to the real decisions of daily life. Our source for the study of Christ's teachings is the Bible, and our starting point is the guideline that includes everything—love.

When Jesus was asked by a man, "What must I do to inherit eternal life?" Jesus responded, "You know the commandments: 'You shall not murder; You shall not commit adultery; You shall not steal; You shall not bear false witness; You shall not defraud; Honor your father and mother'" (Mark 10:17, 19). The commandments that Jesus referred to were accepted by the Jews as God's will; they were expressed to Moses on Mount Sinai (Exodus 20:1–20; Deuter-onomy 5:1–21), and they have stood the test of time as standards of morality for countless generations.

The commandments can also help us understand the true meaning of love. Love is a word used in many ways, and we can deceive ourselves into supposing that our choices arise from love when they do not. The commandments make it clear that murder, adultery, theft, and the like are never the loving thing to do. Jesus did more than affirm the Ten Commandments. He urged us to strive toward the higher standard: "You have heard that it was said to those of ancient times, 'You shall not murder'; and 'whoever murders shall be liable to judgment.' But I say to you that if you are angry with a brother or sister, you will be liable to judgment" (Matthew 5:21–22). He said that we must avoid lustful thoughts, not just adultery. Old patterns allowing divorce, revenge, and hatred must be abandoned in favor of love.

The Pharisees of Jesus' time imposed strict requirements on people with their legal interpretations. When Jesus' disciples were hungry and began to pick heads of grain, the Pharisees accused them of harvesting, forbidden on the Sabbath (Exodus 34:21). Jesus defended his followers on the principle that the Sabbath was made for people and not people for the Sabbath (Mark 2:23–28).

In his teaching, Jesus was urging us to move beyond legalism to what truly fosters love. He said, "Do not think that I have come to abolish the law or the prophets. I have come not to abolish but to fulfill" (Matthew 5:17). Laws are necessary and good, but Christ's followers must constantly strive to view them according to Christ's mind and heart.

Catholics believe that we

Jesus proposed a style of life that was at odds with the prevailing practice in Israel and the Roman Empire. It continues to cut into the societal norms of our age. It has three components:

Sharing goods.

Jesus called for the sharing of surplus goods with the poor. His call to "sell what you have and give to the poor" is a way of setting things right again.

Being servants.

Jesus challenged beliefs about the use of power. "Whoever wishes to become great among you must be your servant, and whoever wishes to be first among you must be slave of all" (Mark 10:43–44).

Standing up for justice.

Jesus' strongest words are aimed at those who abuse authority. "Woe to you Pharisees! For you tithe mint and rue and herbs of all kinds, and neglect justice and the love of God; it is these you ought to have practiced, without neglecting the others" (Luke 11:42).

have another resource available to us as we form our consciences—the teachings of the Church. Jesus is present in his Church and has given its leaders the authority to speak and act in his name. "Whatever you bind on earth," he said to Peter, "will be bound in heaven, and whatever you loose on earth will be loosed in heaven" (Matthew 16:19).

New Testament Christians looked to their leaders for guidance in moral questions, as when the Corinthians wrote to Paul for advice (1 Corinthians 7:1). All New Testament letters offered moral guidance, and some, notably the pastoral letters, gave rules of conduct in matters of Church organization, relationships, and daily life.

Since that time, the Catholic Church has provided moral leadership for its members through laws and instruction from pastors, bishops, and popes. Church leaders are responsible for teaching how the Gospel applies to modern life and for giving us aids such as Catechisms and *The Code of Canon Law* (a collection of laws for the Church) to guide us.

Throughout Church history, there have been great teachers of moral theology like Saint Alphonsus Liguori and great masters of the spiritual life like Saint Teresa of Avila. Their writings have helped form the consciences of generations of Catholics, and they have established moral principles that have been useful for centuries.

Today, there are theologians and spiritual writers who are especially qualified to offer moral guidance by reason of their education and experience. When we are faced with difficult moral decisions, moral theologians and spiritual advisers, past and present, can render valuable assistance and guidance.

The teachings of Jesus Christ and of the Bible, the guidance of the Church, the instructions of moral theologians, and experience are the sources available to us as we strive to form a good conscience. They provide us with objective guidelines so that our decisions are not merely subjective and emotional.

Life for us should be a constant effort to be one with Jesus, making our everyday decisions according to his mind and heart. The way we relate to our family, friends, coworkers, and people on the street should be a result of our relationship with Christ. Our business decisions, political choices, and social relationships should be in harmony with what Christ would do if he were in our place.

HOW We Live It

- *What do you consider a law that is "written" in your heart?*

- *Describe a recent situation where you had to choose between right and wrong. How did you decide what to do?*

- *Choose one of the commandments. How would the world be different if everyone followed this commandment?*

Social Justice Is the Heart of Christianity

The love of Christ will always challenge us to work for peace and social justice and to have a special concern for the poor. Christ cautioned us that our eternal destiny will be determined by our readiness to help others and reminded us that whatever we do for others is done for him (see Matthew 25:31–46).

From the beginning, the Church sought to understand and live out Jesus' command to "love one another as I have loved you" (John 15:12). Just as the practice of charity characterizes the lives of our greatest saints, the call to social responsibility has been a necessary task for the Church, as leaders like Saint Ambrose wrote:

"God created the universe in such a manner that all in common might derive their food from it, and that the earth should also be a property common to all. Why do you reject one who has the same rights over nature as you? It is not from your own goods that you give to the beggar; it is a portion of his own which you are restoring to him. The earth belongs to all."

All Catholic social teaching grows out of the conviction that each one of us has inalienable value because we have been made in God's own image. We are the summit of all creation and destined to spend eternity with God. The human person is entitled to the highest respect and care.

We should care about injustice because God cares about injustice. The sight of the Jewish people enslaved in Egypt was painful to God: "I have observed the misery of my people who are in Egypt; I have heard their cry on account of their taskmasters. Indeed, I know their sufferings, and I have come down to deliver them…" (Exodus 3:7–8).

When God established the people in their own land, each family and tribe received its own parcel of land, because they all were equally God's children. But God knew that, in the course of time, some would lose their land in debt or sickness. Therefore, God established a law that was truly a revolutionary concept.

God proclaimed a Jubilee Year: "And you shall hallow the fiftieth year and you shall proclaim liberty throughout the land to all its inhabitants. It shall be a jubilee for you: you shall return, every one of you, to your property and every one of you to your family….But if there is not sufficient means to recover it, what was sold shall remain with the purchaser until the year of jubilee; in the jubilee it shall be released, and the property shall be returned" (Leviticus 25:10,28). The law of private ownership was clearly superseded here by a higher law, namely, that everyone had a right to the land of the family. If someone lost the land and could not buy it back, that land was to belong to him again each fiftieth year. Thus, there could be no great fortunes built on the backs of the poor.

The modern era of Catholic social thought began with Pope Leo XII's encyclical letter (Rerum Novarum).

Jesus took a stand from the very beginning of his public life. In the synagogue in Nazareth, he read this passage: "The Spirit of the Lord is upon me, because he has anointed me to bring good news to the poor. He has sent me to proclaim release to the captives and recovery of sight to the blind, to let the oppressed go free, to proclaim the year of the Lord's favor" (Luke 4:18–19, see Isaiah 61:1–2). To understand Jesus without taking into account his own very clear descriptions of himself, his ministry, his values, is to miss the point of Jesus. He is not merely an escape from the harshness of this life. Scriptures, instead, show him involved in the pain and anguish of real life.

Jesus did not become a politician, but he was never hesitant to speak out on political issues. The Church tries to follow his example by not avoiding political issues, and this is especially true when human rights are threatened. Jesus' Gospel message was not partisan, but it was political in this way: it concerned itself with people—the way they lived, their freedoms, their inalienable human rights. The Church, therefore, must be a leaven of peace, justice, and equality for all people, an implacable defender of the dignity and rights of God's people.

The modern era of Catholic social thought began

with Pope Leo XIII's encyclical letter, Of New Things (*Rerum Novarum*): On the Condition of Workers (1891). Responding to the great changes in European society that had been brought about by industrialization and urbanization, Pope Leo wrote his letter as a plea for an end to the exploitation of working people. He called for a just and living wage and for the right of workers to organize themselves into unions to bargain collectively. Pope Leo also made it clear that Catholic tradition supported the right to private property and to a fair profit.

The social message of the Church has become more prominent in recent decades not only because of key social encyclicals by popes but because of addressed social issues: "There are people who profess noble sentiments and who in practice, however, are carelessly indifferent to the needs of society" (#30).

The Christian today is called to overcome this "merely individualistic morality." One of the major documents of the Second Vatican Council, the Dogmatic Constitution of the Church in the Modern World, states, "the best way to fulfill one's obligations of justice and love is to contribute to the common good according to one's means and the needs of others, and also to promote

and help public and private organizations devoted to bettering the conditions of life."

The first pillar of Catholic social teaching is the essential dignity of the human person; the second pillar is humanity's social nature. From the moment of conception, we rely on others. First, in the family and, later, as a member of the larger society, each of us depends on others not only for our physical well-being but our moral, intellectual, and spiritual development as well.

Each of us needs society in order to develop our full potential as a human being. Christians need a community of faith to worship and grow close to God. Because of this social dimension, the well-being of society itself is a concern for the Church.

HOW We Live It

- *Why would "good" people ignore suffering people?*
- *What did Jesus say about social justice?*
- *How do we ignore people we don't want to see?*

The Consistent Life Ethic

For most of us there is no problem witnessing to the sacredness of life in particular spheres that touch our hearts in a personal way. A man with a special love for babies is likely to be attracted to the many initiatives designed to protect the unborn. A woman with a horror for war, perhaps coming from her own military experience, may find herself quite naturally working with peace organizations.

The problem is that many of us have areas of what ethical philosophers call value blindness. Because of our upbringing, our experiences, and our cultural conditioning, we may, like a color-blind individual, be unable to see one or the other particular value in its full intensity. For example, someone who was brought up to be self-sufficient might be blind to the truly blameless poverty of those whose disadvantages can only be overcome by outside assistance.

In order to become effective witnesses to a consistent reverence for all life, it is important not only to understand our Church's moral teachings in specific areas but also to explore the kinds of fears that lead to value blindness.

Abortion and the unique preciousness of life

In the face of the millions of abortions performed in the United States since Roe v. Wade, the Church has always taught that abortion is an intrinsically moral evil, that is, an action absolutely opposed to the will of God and the laws of nature and therefore never permissible.

Abortion, when viewed in broad daylight, is easily recognizable as a terrible tragedy. Value blindness sets in, however, when the focus is only on the poor, young, or anxious mother. Then sympathies can cloud over another basic reality: that the very life of the unborn baby is at stake.

This blindness also clouds other realities: the physical, psychological, and spiritual effects of abortion on all the other victims—not only the mother herself but also the father, the siblings, the grandparents, and all who have a connection with this tragedy.

War and the rights of the innocent

To pursue the natural goals of life without fear of aggression is a basic right to which all innocent people are entitled. While Catholic teaching has always allowed for legitimate defensive war to protect the innocent from unjust invasion, the nature of modern war has greatly increased the emphasis on working for peace in all circumstances.

"The development of armaments by modern science has immeasurably magnified the horror and wickedness of war....Every act of war directed to the indiscriminate destruction of whole cities or vast areas with their inhabitants is a crime against God and man, which merits firm and unequivocal condemnation" (The Church in the Modern World, #80).

In spite of such clear statements, fear of totalitarian governments can blind many people to the way warfare policy may push us toward just such destruction of innocent lives. It is of utmost importance that love of innocent life, including the lives of citizens of countries whose governments are aggressive, keep us from considering defensive measures that devalue those innocent lives.

Euthanasia and life's sacredness

Many Christians have become confused about this matter in recent times for two main reasons:

- Modern medical advances have made it possible for many people who would have died in former times to continue living longer in conditions that are burdensome to them or to those who care for them.

- Pro-euthanasia organizations have promoted the idea that death is a basic right for individuals who experience more physical or mental pain than they can bear. From their viewpoint, helping provide "death with dignity" is a noble duty for those who love such an individual.

Catholic magisterial teaching is clear that deliberate killing of the sick or disabled is also an intrinsically moral evil, an action absolutely opposed to the will of God and the laws of nature and, therefore, never permissible. Withholding of ordinary means of treatment such as IVs, food and water, or common surgical procedures in the case of babies or adults with disabilities is also never allowed, unless these means become extraordinary by virtue of unusual circumstances.

On the other hand, there is no obligation on the part of individuals or those caring for them to prolong painful procedures when there is no hope of recovery. Rather than trying to deny sickness and death by a speedy removal of a loved one through euthanasia, the caregivers of the afflicted ones stand by, cherishing their last moments on earth and helping the patients to bear their crosses by sharing in them. At the same time, they can demonstrate their own faith in God's loving promise of eternal life by fostering the sacraments of reconciliation, anointing of the sick, and Eucharist, and then letting go as their loved ones commend themselves into the hands of the Lord.

Capital punishment or mercy

The Catholic Church has always tried to balance justice and mercy in regard to the treatment of crimes of murder. In the case of absolutely clear guilt, justice would make punishment even unto death morally licit. On the other hand, mercy counsels clemency.

In the past, the Church's loving care for perpetrators of even the worst crimes was expressed by praying for and visiting those in prison and ministering the sacraments to them. In recent times, the United States bishops have chosen to place the stress on witnessing to the value of each human life, no matter how guilty the individual may be, by voting against support for state laws allowing capital punishment.

Part of the ongoing reflection concerning capital punishment arose because of changes in historical circumstances. The ability of the state to enforce life imprisonment no longer makes the criminal so much of a threat to society at large.

Catholics concerned about the safety of the innocent and also about witnessing to the absolute value of the life of the criminals are expressing their love of neighbor and efforts to improve family and societal conditions.

HOW We Live It

- *Describe an experience that helped show you the preciousness of every life.*

- *What do you do at home and at work in your community and in your parish to promote a respect for life?*

- *What might be done to help someone who is facing a terminal or chronic illness?*

The Dignity of Life

"All human beings ought to value every person for his or her uniqueness as a creature of God, called to be a brother and sister of Christ," said Pope John Paul II. "This explains our efforts to defend human life against every influence or action that threatens or weakens it."

The U.S. bishops name four priorities for our society's response to the poor:

- The fulfillment of the basic needs of the poor.
- An increase in the active participation in society by the poor and those on society's margins.
- Greater investment of wealth and talent in ways that can directly benefit the poor.
- The evaluation of policies in light of their effect on the poor.

For Catholics, valuing each life goes beyond avoiding taking life to ensuring that each person can live with dignity. The spirituality of Christ demands that we take a stand against anything in society that dehumanizes, represses, or denies rights and dignity.

Economic justice

"Every perspective on economic life that is human, moral, and Christian must be shaped by three questions: What does the economy do for people? What does it do to people? And how do people participate in it?"

With these words, the U.S. Catholic bishops began their 1986 pastoral letter, "Economic Justice for All: Catholic Social Teaching and the U.S. Economy." The bishops insist that economic decisions and activity have a moral dimension because they affect the human person, either enhancing or diminishing human dignity in the process.

In the realm of action, the Church worldwide has a long tradition on which to build—women and men in every age who have given their lives in heroic service to the poor. However, the Church today is asking that we take another step, for "charity requires more than alleviating misery. It demands genuine love for the person in need. It should probe the meaning of suffering and provoke a response that seeks to remedy causes" (Economic Justice for All, #356).

Equality: One Creator, one destiny

All people, regardless of any distinction (race, creed, sex, national origin, sexual orientation, habit of thought, political party, etc.) must be treated with equal dignity. They have been created by God, redeemed by Christ, and are called to spend eternity with God in heaven.

Most agree with such statements about equality. Yet it is quite common to feel some measure of prejudice toward one group or another. According to many psychologists, prejudice is rooted in the human tendency to concentrate our own worst fears and insecurities on another person or a group.

In "Brothers and Sisters to Us," the U.S. Catholic bishops condemned racism as "a radical evil that divides the human family and denies the new creation of a redeemed world." In addition, the bishops ask the Church to boost nonwhite leadership and vocations, foster diversity of liturgical expression, make use of affirmative-action programs, and maintain Catholic schools serving minority communities.

There has been renewal in the Church's ministry to Native Americans through the Tekakwitha Conference, to Hispanics through the national Encuentro gatherings, and to African Americans, most recently, through the National Black Catholic Congress. Efforts like these affirm minority presence within the Church and acknowledge the gifts these cultures bring to the body of Christ.

Equality of female and male

The Second Vatican Council, in its Constitution on the Church in the Modern World, noted that "any kind of social or cultural discrimination in basic personal rights on the grounds of sex, race, color, social conditions, language or religion, must be curbed and eradicated as incompatible with God's design…as is the case with women who are denied the chance freely to choose a husband, or a state of life, or to have access to the same educational cultural benefits as are available to men" (#29).

Pope John Paul II wrote a "meditation" called On the

Dignity and Vocation of Women. Although he was concerned that certain forms of feminism might lead women to become "masculinized" and lose their "essential richness," the pope repeatedly asserted the equality of men and women.

The stewardship of creation

Christian concern for the environment begins with understanding the world as God's gift to us. Our Christian tradition teaches us that we must cherish the gift of creation as we use it for the purpose the Creator intended.

Considered as our most precious gift, creation itself is to be used for the good of all people, according to Catholic social teaching. The Second Vatican Council stated that "God destined the earth and all it contains for all people and nations….In their use of things people should regard the external goods they lawfully possess as not just their own but common to others as well, in the sense that they can benefit others as well as themselves" (The Church in the Modern World).

A distinctive feature of Christian concern for the natural environment is its motivation in gratitude rather than in fear. Certainly, urgent action is needed to correct the imbalances our civilization has created. But if fear alone motivates us, the best we can do is stop harmful activity. Instead, we need to find a way to continue social and economic development so that more and more people may benefit and safeguard the environment.

The world of work and the work of the world

In his 1981 encyclical On Human Work, Pope John Paul II not only reaffirmed the Church's traditional support for unions and for a just wage but also explored anew the significance of work in human life. "Man's life is built up every day from work, from work it derives its specific dignity," wrote the pope. The world of work needs our attention because it can be either a way to build up human beings or destroy them.

Human labor can never be thought of as merely another component of the production process, equal in importance to capital, technology, raw materials, and the like. Labor is not simply something one "sells" in the marketplace like other commodities. The U.S. Catholic bishops wrote, "All work has a threefold moral significance. First, it is a principal way that people exercise the distinctive human capacity for self-expression and self-realization. Second, it is the ordinary way for human beings to fulfill their material needs. Finally, work enables people to contribute to the well-being of the larger community. Work is not only for oneself. It is for one's family, for the nation, and indeed for the benefit of the entire human family" (Economic Justice for All, #97).

HOW We Live It

- *Name an economic decision you were part of recently. How did it help or hurt others?*

- *What groups are the objects of prejudice in your community?*

- *Does society have the obligation to make up for social injustices done to groups of people? If not, why? If so, how?*

Conclude the session by reading Matthew 5:42–45:

Give to everyone who begs from you, and do not refuse anyone who wants to borrow from you. You have heard that it was said, "You shall love your neighbor and hate your enemy." But I say to you, Love your enemies and pray for those who persecute you, so that you may be children of your Father in heaven; for he makes his sun rise on the evil and on the good, and sends rain on the righteous and on the unrighteous.

SUGGESTED RESOURCES

Lukefahr, Oscar. *The Search for Happiness: Four Levels of Emotional and Spiritual Growth.*

Miller, Richard. *We Hold These Truths: Catholicism and American Political Life.*

Various authors. *What Does the Church Teach About ...?* series deals with different aspects of Christian living.

Vomund, Jeffrey. *What Catholics Believe About Lifestyles DVD.*

Concluding Prayer: O God, we thank you for the gift of Church. Help us see ourselves as valuable members of the body of Christ, each with unique gifts and talents that we bring to the community of faith. Open our eyes to the beauty of your work in all people and in all places, and grant us the grace to grow in faith and love. Amen.

SESSION 9

Christian Living: Part Two

WHO gave us some of the most lasting guidelines for discernment, and what are they?

WHAT can help us effectively discern God's will for our lives?

WHERE do Christians find opportunities to do God's work?

WHEN do we know that a decision that we have made is the right one?

WHY is it important to pray about our choices before we make them?

Opening Song: "Blessed Are They," by David Haas, or a hymn of your choice

Opening Prayer: God of all creation, you have called us to this community known as the Catholic Church. Bless our work during this session today, that we may come to better understand who we are and where we come from as members of this Church. Open our minds and our hearts to your word, and to the words of those gathered here with us today. Inspire us with your spirit, and guide us in the way of Jesus, the Christ. Amen.

Reading: Matthew 5:1–12

Spend a moment in quiet reflection.

What Is Holiness?

All of us who are attracted to Jesus Christ have before us the greatest challenge and opportunity possible: to live in his reign and become holy like him.

Suggestions to stimulate your hunger and thirst for holiness

Pray. Ask God to create in you a desire for God and God's kingdom, a desire strong enough to start you irrevocably on your own path toward holiness.

Take definite action. Make a continued effort to be holy. It doesn't really matter whether your actions are large or small. It could mean a change in your lifestyle or the way you do your job. It could mean a habit openly discarded. Whatever it is, do it openly to provide momentum to your desire, to feed and strengthen it.

Ponder the advantages of holiness. Holiness brings peace, release from fear and worry. Holiness is a quality of life that frees you to love and be loved without hindrance. But holiness requires a commitment and a focus on living as Jesus did. Turn your imagination loose, and in a quiet place, think about these things. Write them down if that helps you.

List the current difficulties in your life, and the benefits holiness can bring. Then, beside each item you list put the effect of holiness, of wholeness. For example:

Today Proffers	Holiness Offers
Feelings of fear	Peace, security with God
Conflict with spouse	At-oneness with self and others
Confusion of priorities	Freedom to love
Worry over a job	Desire for holiness in the kingdom

What do you want most in all your experience and dreams? Think about that for a few minutes. Is it something material? Is it related to other people? Is it intangible, hard to express? Is it holiness? Is it God? And this one desire—how much energy, thought, caring, practice goes into it?

Jesus has told us that those who hunger and thirst for holiness will be filled, that blessedness is promised. We have only to desire it—but we must desire it as a starving person desires food.

Many of us have been taught that true holiness is only for saints, for heroes, or only for nuns, priests, and other ministers. But remember, when we look at saints or heroes, we are looking with hindsight. Were they easily saintly? Were they always as holy as we now see them?

They grew as we must grow. Somewhere within them they wanted holiness, and they wanted it very, very much. Their desire for it influenced their decisions. Their desire occupied their minds, changed their feelings. Their desire was an active force in their daily activities.

If we want holiness, we can fill our thoughts with it. We can ponder its beauty. We can long for its results. We can encourage every thought that leads toward the holiness we desire. Our attitudes create actions and circumstances like themselves, becoming visible in our lives. When holiness is our desire, fostered by our thoughts, it will become embodied in our everyday living.

The converse is also true, as Matthew 5:30 reflects: "if your right hand causes you to sin, cut it off and throw it away; it is better for you to lose one of your members than for your whole body to go into hell." Jesus uses the body as a powerful figure of speech. If you want holiness, you will want to get rid of everything and anything that threatens your desire.

If our minds and daily lives are cluttered with countless things that either do not lead us toward holiness or actually lead us away from it, holiness will elude us. But if we clear out the attics within ourselves (or, as Jesus put it, cut off our right hand), there is space and the possibility for holiness.

Goodness does not force itself upon us. We need to invite it, if we want it. Those things we throw out may not be evil at all. For most of us, they are only distractions. But distractions are powerful if they become substitutes for our desire for holiness. If we meander through all the distracting paths of life, we may miss God.

Somewhere within your reach, within yourself, there is a tiny opening. Through that opening is wholeness of life, fullness of loving, fullness of peace, fullness of joy. You can have it. It is your birthright as a human being, a child of God. God has not made it difficult. You and I have made it difficult by cluttering up our inner selves.

But you can find the way and get past the self-made obstacles. You can follow the path to the opening into life. That path is not wide and obvious, but it is there. It begins right where you are at this moment.

HOW We Live It

- *Figure out how much time you spend on various things each day. According to the amounts of time you spend, what do you desire most?*

- *Name something that gets in the way of your desire for holiness. What can you do about changing this situation?*

- *Do you know anyone you would consider holy?*

Discernment

Life is full of decisions, big and small, and sometimes it's difficult to know exactly what God is asking of us. Yet divine guidance in making these decisions is available to all of us.

The decision-making process—often called discernment—can be a rather complex process due to our lack of self-knowledge, our lack of inner freedom, and our great ability to try to have God say "yes" to what we want. Yet none of this should discourage us.

As Christians, because the Holy Spirit lives in our hearts (see 1 Corinthians 6:19), we believe that we can indeed come to a good sense of God's truth for our lives. With the Holy Spirit on our side and with a willingness to learn—through reading, through talking with other mature Christians, and especially through trial-and-error—we can grow in our ability to recognize and discern the voice of God from voices that are not of the Lord.

There are no foolproof ways that will lead us to absolute certainty concerning God's will in a particular situation, but there are specific guidelines that can help us to grow in our ability to perceive and discern God's call and action in our lives. Saint Ignatius of Loyola gave us some of the most lasting guidelines in his spiritual exercises. As we grow in the art and gift of discernment, we will develop a method that works best for us.

What can help us effectively discern God's will for us?

Living a God-centered life

Personal knowledge of God and God's ways

Reflective living

Genuine openness to God

Self knowledge

Here are seven steps that are based on Ignatius' guidelines

1. Formulate a proposition

Start by making a clear statement or question of what you are trying to decide. For example, "Should I change careers?" "Should I terminate my relationship with so-and-so?" "Should I join a particular ministry in my parish?" From the beginning and right through the process, ask God to reveal God's truth to you and give you the inner freedom to carry it out.

2. Gather the relevant information

Reflect on the various alternatives, and the advantages and disadvantages of each. For example, there may be more options available than just quitting or continuing a job or relationship. Perhaps it is possible to continue in a job or relationship but work toward (or even demand) some definite changes.

Identify potential obstacles. What excessive needs, attachments, and compulsions might prevent your hearing God's word and doing God's will? To what extent are you attached to one particular alternative? How free are you to embrace any alternative or direction if you believe it is God's will for you?

It is helpful to seek out a good counselor, whether a wise spiritual director or friend, preferably one who knows you well.

3. Bring the gathered information to prayer

The heart of Christian discernment is not the intellectual activity of weighing the pros and cons of available options, but rather, the act of bringing the available options to prayer and seeing which option gives you the greatest sense of God's presence, peace, and joy.

Often we are so attached to a particular direction that we are not free to move in another direction—hence, the vital importance of praying for the grace of inner freedom.

We are at the point of inner freedom when we are detached enough from every available option to be free to walk down any path that God may call us to walk. Ideally, you should not choose a particular option until you are free to embrace every available option. This part of the discernment process is the most important and the most challenging.

When you have attained, through the grace of God, a good degree of inner freedom, you then begin to pray about the various options available to you. The option that consistently fills you with the presence of God's peace and joy over a period of time is most likely God's will for you.

As part of this third step, Saint Ignatius suggests three imaginative exercises.

- First, consider what advice you would give to another person faced with the same situation.

- Second, imagine yourself on your deathbed and ask what you would then wish to have chosen.

- Third, picture yourself standing before God on the last day and consider what decision you would then wish to have made.

These exercises will help you distance yourself from the decision facing you and to look at it with some objectivity.

4. Make a decision

At some point, you must make a decision. You should go with the option that gives you the most peace when you are in prayer.

If you don't experience real peace about any of the options available to you, postpone the decision or choose the one that is least troublesome. Don't decide if you are in doubt; continue to pray until you experience peace about a particular option.

Be aware that the option chosen may not always be the most attractive one or the one you most desired. Sometimes you may feel led to choose an option with tears—for example, to return to a marriage situation that in the past caused much pain. Such initial tears of sadness, however, often give way to tears of joy (See 2 Corinthians 7:8–13).

5. Live with the decision

Once you come to a decision, live with it for a while before you actually act on what you decided. Your decision may involve a major change in your life, and you may need time to adjust and begin the process.

6. Act on the decision

This may seem obvious, but this step can be the most difficult because it may involve giving up something to which you are still quite attached. Ask the Holy Spirit to give you the courage to act on what you believe to be God's will for your life.

7. Seek confirmation of the decision

The final test for hearing God's will is whether living it out brings life to you and to others. If the choice you make bears good fruit, you can be quite sure you acted in accord with God's will. This is not to say that there won't be struggles connected with your choice or days when you will wonder, "Did I really make the right choice?" Such struggles and wondering are normal and do not necessarily mean that you made a wrong decision.

Discernment is not just a gift but an art learned through trial and error. God doesn't ask that we always be right; God asks only that we always try to be honest and act out of our best understanding of a particular situation.

HOW We Live It

- *How do you usually make decisions? Do you follow your head or your heart? Do you write down options or seek the advice of others?*

- *What other "voices" besides God's influence your decisions?*

- *Recall an important decision that you made in your life. How has it turned out? Can you see the hand of God acting in that decision?*

Evangelization

Evangelization is as old as Christianity itself. Christ's last words to us before ascending into heaven were about evangelizing: "Go, therefore, and make disciples of all nations, baptizing them in the name of the Father and of the Son and of the Holy Spirit, and teaching them to obey everything that I have commanded you" (Matthew 28:19–20).

Evangelization involves much more than bringing the Gospel to people who have never heard the Good News. It also means bringing Christians to a deeper awareness of Christ touching their lives. Through evangelization, hearers of the word of God become better equipped to become doers of the word. Thus, evangelization forms the basis for all ministry within the Church.

In 2004, there were more than twenty million inactive Catholics in the United States and more than eighty million unchurched Americans. As Catholics, we need to recover an awareness of that primary call from Jesus to share the faith.

Here is a five-step plan for evangelization based on the teachings of Pope Paul VI in his apostolic exhortation, On Evangelization in the Modern World (all quotes are from this document).

1. Witness Christ

Our first step in becoming evangelizers is to live lives that witness our faith in Christ. "Modern people listen more readily to witnesses than to teachers. If they listen to teachers, it is because they are witnesses." The positive witness of a loving, caring, and forgiving Catholic is the strongest method of attracting people to Jesus and to the Church. No one should feel like a stranger in our midst. We should be a welcoming Church.

2. Share your faith

Silent witness is not enough, "for witness, no matter how excellent, will ultimately prove ineffective unless its meaning is clarified and corroborated….The meaning of a person's witness will be clarified by preaching, clearly and unambiguously, the Lord Jesus." Jesus was the greatest witness who ever lived, yet his witness would not have reached us had he not ceaselessly explained what salvation meant for daily life. His Sermon on the Mount, his parables, and his dialogues with people show us how to share what we believe with others.

3. Offer the option for love

Pope John Paul II told America's youth on a pastoral visit to the United States, "I offer you the option for love, the option for Christ….To evangelize is to witness to God revealed in Jesus Christ, in the Spirit."

The best way to do this is on a person-to-person basis. People attract people. Love begets love. Faith in action becomes love, and love takes the shape of service. The greatest service we can give is to offer Christ's invitation to salvation from death and sin through a life of love, justice, and mercy.

Here are some ways you can Engage in Evangelization

Pray. Ask God to whom you should reach out: a neighbor, a co-worker, the grocery checker, a member of your family.

Take steps to know the persons who are in need of evangelization. Look for their spiritual needs, find ways to approach them, and meet those needs.

Listen to the people God brings into your life. Your attentiveness can open up many possibilities to witness to your own faith, both in word and deed.

Begin a Bible study or faith-sharing group in your neighborhood or at work.

Initiate an adult discussion group to give alienated Catholics an opportunity to talk about issues that concern them.

Visit hospitals, shut-ins, nursing homes, and prisons. These people need your encouraging words, concerned presence, or thoughtful signs of love and caring.

4. Challenge our culture

Our Catholic witness should affect the values of our society and challenge us to be counter-cultural when necessary. Evangelization involves upsetting values, lines of thought, and models of life that contradict the Word of God and the plan of salvation.

Jesus asks us to bring the Gospel to bear on our society. He asks us to speak up on behalf of the poor and the homeless, to strengthen the place of marriage and family in our society, and to raise our children with respect for the virtue of nonviolence. We cannot segregate our religious life from life in our culture, for the hidden energy of the Gospel has the power to transform culture.

5. Make the good better

Culture must be regenerated by an encounter with the Gospel. This is our Christian responsibility. We must do what we can to see that advances in medicine be used at the service of life and not for abortion or euthanasia; to make certain that tax dollars that support a massive defense establishment be used to maintain peace in the world; and to find ways to move our economic system toward benefiting members of our society and the world who depend upon us.

What is good in our culture can be better when touched by the transforming power of Christ's Good News. Our Church did this with a pagan Roman Empire, barbarian hordes, and the unbelievers in the Enlightenment. We can do it again for the technological culture of our time. Vatican II said we should face the modern world with joy and hope, with the optimism of the transforming Gospel. When all is said and done, the first audience for evangelization is the active Catholic. Convinced Catholics will convince others. Caring Catholics will attract others. Our conversion is more than a once-in-a-lifetime event or the peak experience of being "born again."

Evangelization is more than a program; it is a process. Christ's call to build his Church must be offered again and again to Catholics as we go through our life stages. When we are evangelized, we will evangelize others.

HOW We Live It

- *Describe a person who helped introduce Catholicism to you.*

- *Name something "good" about our culture. How could that good thing be made better in Christ's service?*

- *What can you do to evangelize your parish?*

Called to Build God's Kingdom

The word "layperson" describes God's high calling to faith and to service. A layperson is an adopted child of God, a sister or brother of Jesus, and an heir to God's wealth of grace and life eternal, called to build God's kingdom here on earth.

Being a layperson means being a member of the "priesthood of the faithful." Lay Christians often hesitate to use the word "priests" when referring to themselves; and yet that is what they are: "But you are a chosen race, a royal priesthood, a holy nation, God's own people, in order that you may proclaim the mighty acts of him who called you out of darkness into his marvelous light" (1 Peter 2:9).

Though the average Catholic associates priesthood with those who are ordained by a bishop, a kind of priesthood has already been bestowed on those who have received baptism. Christ sends his faithful ones into the world to transform the values of societies and individuals into those of the kingdom of God, to minister to people as he, himself, would minister.

Before his passion and death, he prayed for all his disciples, present and future. "They do not belong to the world, just as I do not belong to the world. Sanctify them in the truth; your word is truth. As you have sent me into the world, so I have sent them into the world" (John 17:16–18).

Christ identifies his disciples with himself, as citizens of heaven. As a body, they are united with the Father to the same degree the Son is united with the Father and the Holy Spirit in perfect unity.

The priesthood of the faithful is made up of married, single, celibate religious, and widowed men and women, each with special gifts and opportunities to serve, according to each one's state in life. All people should earnestly seek to develop the qualities and talents bestowed on them in accord with these conditions of life.

Married persons have a primary responsibility to be living signs of Christ's love for the Church through their sacramental relationship of marriage. It is important, therefore, that marriage preparation should emphasize the various spiritual as well as emotional, social, sexual, and economic aspects of Christian marriage.

The single life, whether for a period of time or for a lifetime, is a special call within the priesthood of the faithful. Many single persons may have the time to devote to youth ministry, the elderly or the sick, evangelization, religious education, or administration of programs. A single person not vowed to celibacy, but actually living a celibate life, might consider the possibility of living in community with other single adults who have different careers but who gather for prayer, support, and Christian witness.

The widowed have a special place in the life of the Church due to their ability to help others who experience grief and loss. Those who were widowed when older have a special place due to their wisdom and years of experience. There are opportunities for them to serve the sick, elderly, shut-ins, families, and youth, as well as to attend daily Mass and other devotions.

For the Christian, the whole world is full of opportunities to do God's work.

At home. Since many of the priesthood of the laity are called to the vocation of married life, they are also called to family life. Thus, their primary responsibilities revolve around spouse and children; other kinds of service in the Church come second. "Christian couples are, for each other, for their children and for their relatives, cooperators of grace and witnesses of the faith. They are the first to pass on the faith to their children and to educate them in it. By word and example they form them to a Christian and apostolic life" (Decree on the Laity, #11).

At work. Ordinary daily work offers opportunities to glorify God and witness to God's love. The ways in which Christian laity perform their daily chores can be a powerful witness to the grace of God. "On life's pilgrimage…generously they exert all their energies in extending God's kingdom, in making the Christian spirit a vital energizing force in the temporal sphere" (Decree on the Laity, #4).

Sharing Christ in the workplace is a sensitive issue, since Christian charity demands we respect the beliefs of others. In no way should we push our beliefs on others. Christ himself invited people to believe in him and let the Spirit do the rest. But there will be times when an explicit explanation of the life and work of Jesus Christ will be in order.

At church. While liturgical ministries such as lector, extraordinary minister of Communion, and so forth, are perhaps the most visible lay ministries, they are no more important than service to shut-ins, setting up the hall for parish socials, or serving refreshments. Welcoming other members of the parish at Mass, participating in social and educational activities, and participating in outreach opportunities are other ways to connect with the parish and build the kingdom of God.

For others. Finally, one can exercise the priesthood of the faithful among friends, extended family, and community, by seeking opportunities to reconcile and build bridges between the Church and various groups and organizations: "That is the attempt to infuse with the Christian spirit the mentality and behavior, laws and structures of the community in which one lives. So much is it the special work and responsibility of lay people that it cannot be properly carried out by any others" (Decree on the Laity, #13).

The call to the priestly building of God's kingdom begins with faith, which is more than trust in God's promises or emotional experiences. Faith is both a gift from God and a personal assent to the person, life, and teachings of Jesus Christ as proposed by the Church.

The laity cannot be effective if they are not educated and constantly updated in their faith. For this reason, the Church encourages all adults to be involved in ongoing spiritual formation, a process by which God forms a person more and more into God's divine image, as a potter forms clay into beautiful vessels.

Spiritual formation best takes place within the context of a believing community, usually the local parish. The life of the parish is centered on the Eucharist and the celebration of the other sacraments, as well as on good preaching and teaching, thus forming a solid basis for strengthening growth in faith and in knowledge about Christ's teachings.

One way formation can occur is in small groups. Here, the laity may share personal concerns, insights, and inspirations. Even Jesus seems to have needed his small group: Peter, James, and John were present for many of the Lord's most intimate moments.

Another kind of spiritual formation is spiritual direction with an "elder" in the faith, whether cleric, religious, or lay.

Finally, self-directed formation that can take place during regular times of prayer, Scripture study, and reading of good spiritual literature by respected authors is important for spiritual growth.

If laypeople recognize their dignity, mission, and ministry as members of the priesthood of the faithful, the Church will be better able to win the world to Christ.

HOW We Live It

- *How do you build the kingdom of God in your life?*

- *As a citizen of heaven, what are your rights? What are your responsibilities?*

- *In what way are you indispensable to Christ's Church?*

Conclude the session with the Suscipe, written by Saint Ignatius Loyola:

Take, Lord, receive all my liberty,
my memory, my understanding and my entire will.
You have given all to me; now I return it.
Dispose of it according to your will.
Give me only your love and your grace.
That is enough for me.

SUGGESTED RESOURCES

Allen, John L. Jr. *Global Good News: Unseen Work of the Catholic Church.*

D'Avila-Latourrette, Victor-Antoine. *Simply Living the Beatitudes.*

Keating, James. *Listening for Truth: Praying Our Way to Virtue.*

Redemptorist Fathers. *Handbook for Today's Catholic Family: Revised Edition.*

Concluding Prayer: O God, we thank you for the gift of Church. Help us see ourselves as valuable members of the body of Christ, each with unique gifts and talents that we bring to the community of faith. Open our eyes to the beauty of your work in all people and in all places, and grant us the grace to grow in faith and love. Amen.

SESSION 10

Prayer

WHO should we talk to as a friend or confidant when we pray?

WHAT are five prayer forms that are a part of Catholic practice?

WHERE can we turn to find God's replies/responses to our prayers?

WHEN is it good to pray and when is it OK not to pray?

WHY do Catholics use and repeat certain traditional prayers?

Opening Song: "Peace Prayer," by Sebastian Temple, or a hymn of your choice

Opening Prayer: God of all creation, you have called us to this community known as the Catholic Church. Bless our work during this session today, that we may come to better understand who we are and where we come from as members of this Church. Open our minds and our hearts to your word, and to the words of those gathered here with us today. Inspire us with your spirit, and guide us in the way of Jesus, the Christ. Amen.

Reading: Matthew 6:6–15

Spend a moment in quiet reflection.

Catholics and Prayer

Catholics are encouraged to pray frequently—not only when they are in church but at other times as well: at home, out walking, or in a favorite quiet place. Prayer is a bit like friendship. If you asked friends why they spend time together, they'd probably say, "We just like being together."

It's the same with prayer. At its heart, prayer is a relationship—our relationship with God. Saint Teresa of Avila said, "Prayer in my opinion is nothing else than an intimate sharing between friends; it means taking time frequently to be alone with God who loves us."

Talking with God can be like talking with a friend or confidant. What are some of the things you would say to someone who is close to you? These are things you can and should tell God. Use your own words to say what you want sincerely and honestly. You can thank God, compliment God, tell God you're sorry, or simply talk about your life. Sometimes that might even mean grumbling to God.

But there's another important part of prayer: We also need to listen to God. You won't hear with your ears, but you'll "hear" with your heart. Inspirations and the feeling that God is close are some ways God might speak to you.

There are five prayer forms that are part of Catholic practice:

Prayers of adoration acknowledge that we are God's holy creation, and exalt the greatness of the God who made us.

Prayers of petition recognize that we are sinners who ask God's forgiveness.

Intercessory prayer is our request that God respond to the needs of others. We act as Jesus did when he spoke to the Father in prayer.

Prayers of thanksgiving reflect our joy at the many gifts God has given us, and respond to the forgiveness we receive when we turn away from God.

Prayers of praise acknowledge God for his own sake, celebrating God's divinity and mastery over all.

Sometimes we don't know what to say in our prayers, or maybe it is difficult to stay focused on God. That's why knowing some *traditional prayers* can be helpful. (You'll find some of them at the end of this lesson.) Repeating a prayer helps to focus attention on God and still the mind.

Traditional prayers help if you don't know what to say. You probably have used the words "I love you" to show your feelings for those you care about. Millions have used the same words, because those words are often the best way to express a feeling. Catholics repeat certain prayers because they have found they are the best way to express certain thoughts to God.

There is another advantage to repeating prayers. What if you got together a band and everybody played a different song? But when they start playing the same song, it can be the most beautiful experience on earth. It's the same with prayer. When the people join together, speaking to God in the same words, it can be a beautiful expression of our union together as a Church and as sisters and brothers in Christ.

Contemplative prayer is the deepest prayer of all. You begin where you are and allow God to draw you with the Spirit into your own heart.

Here are basic directions for one type of contemplative prayer:

Find a place of quiet. Protect yourself from interruption (close the door, turn off the phone, and so forth). Be comfortable.

Begin by asking God to guide and bless your contemplation.

Start to notice your breathing. The Bible says God breathed God's own breath into us at creation (See Genesis 2:7). It is your very life; it is holy. Observe it with appreciation.

As you become quieter inside, you may repeat a prayer word or phrase. It may be a holy name, like Jesus or Mary. It may be a quality, like love or peace. Focus on this prayer word, repeat it mentally, and let your mind follow it.

Allow yourself to be more and more still, while becoming more and more aware. God is in that stillness, and you will be met there.

When thoughts distract you, do not get involved in them. Turn your attention gently back to your prayer word. If you "come to" and realize you've been far away in your thoughts, be kind to yourself and return to your prayer word.

Keep it simple. Be gentle. Be open to God, who loves you.

You may wish to begin with fifteen or twenty minutes each day, or twice a day. Practicing at the same time every day can help. With a little practice, you will begin to notice that something is definitely going on within you—perhaps beyond your ordinary awareness. Trust that! God begins where you allow God to act.

Contemplative prayer takes you beyond the chattering mind and into the heart, where God dwells. However good your thoughts may be, go beyond them to the stillness, a foretaste of eternity, and there meet our God. One day you will perceive something of God in the silence of your heart. Do you wonder what it will be? Practice contemplation and see.

HOW We Live It

- *How do you best pray? With your own words? With traditional prayers? With Scripture?*

- *What are some thoughts that have come to you during prayer?*

- *What is your image of God when you pray? Do you see yourself in an intimate relationship with God, or is it more distant?*

Jump-starting Your Prayer Life

Sometimes we don't like to pray. Sometimes we are less interested in prayer than in everything else we do. There may be times in our lives when we love to pray, but just as often, we may avoid it or minimize the time we spend. Since the quality of our prayer experience will not always be the same—its flavor will range from dry toast to the richest cream sauce—how can we make our prayer life come alive? Here are some ideas to explore.

Invest more, not less

One way to help prayer become more interesting is to throw ourselves into it anew, devoting more energy to it than before. We may bring to prayer a steadier attention. We may speak to God more intimately and tell God straight out what we are thinking and feeling. We may make prayer an ongoing project of our lives. That means including prayer in all our activities—mowing the lawn, sitting in traffic, making love, talking to children—all of it.

Pray only when you want to

Discipline and duty have their place. But when we are trying to make our prayer come alive, it is wise to notice when we feel like praying, to pray then and not push ourselves into it at other times. If we ask God to teach us to enjoy prayer, the Spirit will plant the impulse toward prayer in our hearts. If we pay attention to that impulse and honor it by praying—maybe for only a few seconds—we will be drawn more and more to God.

Read Scripture frequently

Sometimes praying is like trying to communicate with a stranger. The study of Scripture turns that "stranger"—God—into an acquaintance, then a friend, and finally a loved master. Often the very words of the Bible suddenly take on life, and we experience a oneness with the Creator. We gain not only a greater understanding but also an awareness of the presence of God. In that moment, we are at prayer.

Pray spontaneously

This means thinking or speaking to God without particular preparation, just as we speak to one another. Asking, "God, what do you want here?" is a very different experience from saying, "I wonder what God would think about this." In spontaneous prayer, we talk to God any time, any place, even without a reason. As thinking "to God" instead of "about God" becomes habitual, prayer begins to seep into all of life instead of being reserved for particular times and places.

Be aware of God's responses

God does not necessarily communicate with us in the ways we may expect. We need to remain open, attentive. Look at events: Is God's reply hidden here? Listen for hints in conversations or reading. Perhaps a sentence will strike our heart with peculiar clarity. We may have intuitive awareness that something is shifting, either inside ourselves or in our circumstances. When we think we have "heard" God's reply, we can then act on it.

Try new forms of prayer

Pray with your body alone. The advantage of bodily prayer is that it is wordless and can involve all aspects of ourselves. You may want to begin with hand gestures only, then add arms, head, and little by little, the rest of your body. Look inside yourself, touch the feeling you want to express to God. Then, in that impulse, allow your body to move as it will and offer this movement to God.

Sing your prayer. You may sing to the Lord familiar songs you know and love. Or you may sing/chant spontaneously, using your own words and melody. God does not care about operatic qualities. God cares about the heart. If singing to God enlivens your heart, then do it!

Write your prayer. Writing is a lovely expression of your thoughts and feelings to God. Selections from your journal can also be shared with friends, faith-sharing groups, or family. If writing your prayers makes your own prayer more vital, start a journal!

Image your prayer. Saint Ignatius of Loyola bases much of his teaching about spiritual life on imagery. Ignatius' recommendation is to read a Scripture passage slowly, especially the stories about Jesus, then make pictures of it and imagine yourself in them. Let the story unfold with Jesus and you both present.

Pray the newspaper. Pray for and about the people and situations in the news, giving thanks for the good and begging help for those who are in misery. This type of prayer relates the world to God and allows us to be compassionate with the joys and sufferings of our family throughout the world.

Offer your life as prayer. We can offer our thoughts, words, actions—indeed, the very essence of who we are—not only in special times of prayer but a thousand times a day, in the midst of anything and everything. Soon we are living in God's presence most of the time and offering our very self to God without pause.

Pray your gratitude. Brother David Steindl-Rast, OSB, makes thankfulness the centerpiece of all his prayer and his living. He says that every evening he thanks God for at least one thing he's never thanked God for before. When you cultivate a grateful heart, not only prayer but all of life may be suffused with amazement and praise.

Cultivate wonder. Start with something simple, like a flower, or something you already love, like a song or the moon. Be quiet with it for a bit. Then begin to admire it, marvel at it, revel in its beauty. Try a brief moment of wonder every day. Pause at ordinary events and allow yourself to become more fully aware of them. Savor the preciousness of each experience and of each person.

Pray with nature. Nature deepens us wherever we are. Find a place where you can appreciate and enjoy the green of the earth, the blue of the sky, the smell of salt air or flowers blooming—any aspect of the natural world that fills you with peace and wonder at the beauty of God's creation.

If we want a relationship with God that is vivid in our experience, exciting for our living, and supportive of our very self, then prayer is the most direct way to that relationship. If we long for communication with God, prayer is the means, whatever form we choose.

HOW We Live It

- *How do you feel about your prayer life?*
- *What steps can you take to change it, whether to deepen your relationship with God or enliven the way you pray?*
- *Describe a time when God answered your prayer in a way that wasn't obvious.*

The Lord's Prayer: Jesus' Gift to Us

Our Father, who art in heaven,
hallowed be thy name;
thy kingdom come, thy will be done
on earth as it is in heaven.
Give us this day our daily bread;
and forgive us our trespasses;
as we forgive those who trespass against us;
and lead us not into temptation,
but deliver us from evil. Amen.

The Lord's Prayer provides Christians with rich possibilities for reflection and spiritual growth. Tertullian, one of the early Church Fathers, notes that the Lord's Prayer "is truly the summary of the whole Gospel."

According to Jesus' teaching, the most important issue is attitude. "And whenever you pray, do not be like the hypocrites; for they love to stand and pray in the synagogues and at the street corners, so that they may be seen by others. Truly I tell you, they have received their reward. But whenever you pray, go into your room and shut the door and pray to your Father in secret; and your Father who sees in secret will reward you" (Matthew 6:5–6).

Say the Lord's Prayer slowly, pausing after each phrase. Allow each phrase to sink deeply into your innermost being. Breathe one word or line of the Lord's Prayer between inhalation and exhalation. As you do so, visualize God's love flowing into you more deeply with each breath.

Our Father, who art in heaven...

Jesus spoke of God as "Abba." When Jesus addressed his Father this way, he was essentially saying "Daddy." By inviting us to call God "Abba," Jesus reveals to us that we too have a special relationship with God as God's children.

The psalms tell us why we should praise God. God "is gracious and merciful" and "near to all who call on him" for help. God is one who "gives food to the hun-gry," "heals the brokenhearted," and "binds up their wounds."

Imagine God, like a loving parent, holding you close, telling you how deeply you are loved. As a child rests in the arms of a loving parent, relax in the embrace of your loving God.

Hallowed be thy name; thy kingdom come...

Jesus has given each of us a mission for the kingdom of God: "Go into all the world and proclaim the good news to the whole creation" (Mark 16:15).

What specific gift is Jesus inviting you to use in building the kingdom of God? What is your specific mission? Spend time sharing with Jesus your response to his invitation. Decide what steps you want to take in order to become more Christlike in your own attitudes, and pray for the courage to take the first step.

Thy will be done on earth as it is in heaven...

We believe that Jesus came to reveal the depths of God's boundless love. God's will for you is to open yourself to the reality of this love. All your joys, sufferings, and failures are like a splendid tapestry—each thread is connected to and forms an intricate part of the whole.

What changes do you need to make in your life to bring it into conformity with God's will? What are the obstacles to doing God's will? What steps do you need to take to bring about a greater openness to God's will? Spend time discussing these questions in a loving dialogue with God.

Give us this day our daily bread...

According to some biblical scholars, in this phrase Jesus seems to be calling on us to trust in divine providence to take care of our needs.

Spend some time in intercessory prayer, asking God to give joy, peace, love, and strength to yourself and others as you build God's kingdom. Picture Christ holding each person and intention in his heart. As you pray, lift up the needs of the world, the nation, and the Church, as well as your personal intentions. Jesus is present in the world through our presence to our sisters and brothers.

Forgive us our trespasses; as we forgive those who trespass against us...

In order to be forgiven by God, the Christian must be willing to forgive the offenses of others. Sometimes forgiveness begins with a decision to want to forgive, and it may take time for a deep healing to occur. Be patient with the process and continue to trust that you will be able to forgive by the power of God's forgiving love within you.

If you have difficulty forgiving someone, try this suggestion. Take time to relax and quiet yourself. Ask God to take from you any impediment that might block you from forgiving another. Take your time as you get in touch with any feelings that might block you, turning over each obstacle to God. Visualize God as a bright light radiating warmth, forgiveness, and love into your heart. Visualize the light slowly expanding, surrounding the person you need to forgive with forgiveness and love.

And lead us not into temptation, but deliver us from evil.

It is so easy for us to get lost, to fail, to slip into a sudden weakness. When we are empty, aware of our own sins, weaknesses, and failures, God can touch, free, deliver, heal, and fill us.

The peace that Jesus offers his followers is his own peace, which flows from his intimate communion with Abba. The peace that Jesus gives us does not leave us during difficult times of poverty, suffering, oppression, temptation, or illness. Jesus carries us, lifting us up into the arms of our Abba. There we encounter the love that surpasses all understanding, sustaining us in the midst of darkness and misunderstanding, fear and human weakness.

Reflect on the times in your life in which Jesus lifted you up. Share with Jesus your thoughts and feelings about those times. Now visualize God's love going ahead of you to a future experience, filling that time with light, healing, courage, joy, peace, and love. Remember, Jesus will always be there to carry you and lift you up.

HOW We Live It

- *How can you make Jesus present in the world through your presence to others?*

- *What worries keep you from seeking first the kingdom of God in your life? Share these worries with God, and ask God to help you set your heart on the kingdom first.*

- *How are you being challenged to trust God at this point in your life? Does the Lord's Prayer have a particular insight to offer you in this regard?*

Traditional Catholic Prayers

Along with the Lord's Prayer, these are the five basic prayers that people say outside the liturgy. These prayer formulas are used alone and in combination at many Catholic functions that call for prayer.

The Sign of the Cross

In the name of the Father, and of the Son,
and of the Holy Spirit. Amen.

This prayer dates back to the second century, when Christians would trace the sign of the cross on their foreheads with their thumbs so that they could recognize each other during times of persecution. Taking the right hand and touching it to your forehead, breast, left shoulder, and then right shoulder, make the Sign of the Cross. It is the traditional way Catholics begin and end their prayers.

The Hail Mary

Hail Mary, full of grace. The Lord is with you.
Blessed are you among women,
and blessed is the fruit of your womb, Jesus.
Holy Mary, Mother of God, pray for us sinners,
now and at the hour of our death. Amen.

The Hail Mary begins with two biblical verses, translations of the words of the Archangel Gabriel: "Greetings, favored one! The Lord is with you" (Luke 1:28) and the words of Mary's cousin Elizabeth, "Blessed are you among women, and blessed is the fruit of your womb" (Luke 1:42). It concludes with a petition for intercession that acknowledges Mary as the Mother of our Savior.

From prayer texts of the earliest centuries, the Hail Mary gradually became a popular prayer by the end of the twelfth century, and its recitation was officially urged and encouraged.

The Little Doxology

Glory be to the Father, and to the Son,
and to the Holy Spirit, as it was in the beginning,
is now, and ever shall be, world without end.
Amen.

A doxology is a prayer of praise and gratitude to God. This traditional Catholic doxology is what is known as the "Glory Be." The Greater Doxology is the Gloria recited at Mass.

The Apostles' Creed

I believe in God, the Father almighty,
creator of heaven and earth.
I believe in Jesus Christ, his only Son, our Lord.
He was conceived by the power of the Holy Spirit
and born of the Virgin Mary.
He suffered under Pontius Pilate,
was crucified, died, and was buried.
He descended to the dead.
On the third day he rose again.
He ascended into heaven, and is seated
at the right hand of the Father.
He will come again to judge
the living and the dead. I believe in the Holy Spirit,
the holy catholic Church,
the communion of saints,
the forgiveness of sins,
the resurrection of the body,
and the life everlasting. Amen.

The Apostles' Creed was a variation of an ancient Roman creed. In the Reformation period, Martin Luther, Calvin, and Zwingli recognized it as a basic statement of Christian beliefs. It is thought that this creed, as opposed to the more detailed and precisely worded Nicene Creed used in the Roman liturgy, might be an instrument of Church unity.

The Rosary

Another popular prayer form is the rosary, which is a meditation on events in the life of Jesus and Mary. It uses the Sign of the Cross, the Apostles' Creed, the Our Father, the Hail Mary, and the Glory Be as a framework. For those times when we want to pray but find it difficult or impossible in our own words, the rosary is a great help.

Many people like to pray the rosary while reflecting on a group of mysteries that highlight an aspect of Jesus and Mary's life.

HOW TO PRAY THE ROSARY

1. Make the sign of the cross and say the Apostles' Creed.
2. Say the Our Father.
3. Say three Hail Marys.
4. Say the Glory Be to the Father.
5. Say the Our Father.
6. Say ten Hail Marys.
7. Say the Glory Be.
8. Repeat steps 5, 6, and 7, continuing through all five decades—each set of ten beads.

The Joyful Mysteries

The Annunciation. "You will conceive in your womb and bear a son, and you will name him Jesus" (Luke 1:31).

The Visitation. "Mary set out and went with haste to a Judean town in the hill country, where she entered the house of Zechariah and greeted Elizabeth" (Luke 1:39–40).

The Birth of Christ. "And she gave birth to her firstborn son and wrapped him in bands of cloth, and laid him in a manger, because there was no place for them in the inn" (Luke 2:7).

The Presentation. "When the time came for their purification according to the law of Moses, they brought him up to Jerusalem to present him to the Lord" (Luke 2:22).

The Finding of Jesus in the Temple. "After three days they found him in the temple, sitting among the teachers, listening to them and asking them questions" (Luke 2:46).

The Sorrowful Mysteries

The Agony in the Garden. "Then Jesus went with them to a place called Gethsemane" (Matthew 26:36).

The Scourging at the Pillar. "Then they spat in his face and struck him; and some slapped him, saying, 'Prophesy to us, you Messiah! Who is it that struck you?'" (Matthew 26:67–68).

The Crowning With Thorns. "And after twisting some thorns into a crown, they put it on his head. They put a reed in his right hand" (Matthew 27:29).

The Carrying of the Cross. "So they took Jesus; and carrying the cross by himself, he went out to what is called The Place of the Skull" (John 19:16–17).

The Crucifixion. "Jesus, crying with a loud voice, said, 'Father, into your hands I commend my spirit'" (Luke 23:46).

The Glorious Mysteries

The Resurrection. "He is not here; for he has been raised" (Matthew 28:6).

The Ascension. "So then the Lord Jesus, after he had spoken to them, was taken up into heaven and sat down at the right hand of God" (Mark 16:19).

The Descent of the Holy Spirit. "All of them were filled with the Holy Spirit" (Acts 2:4).

The Assumption of Mary into Heaven. "You have done all this with your own hand…and God is well pleased with it. May the Almighty Lord bless you forever" (Judith 15:10).

The Coronation of Mary. "A great portent appeared in heaven: a woman clothed with the sun, with the moon under her feet, and on her head a crown of twelve stars" (Revelation 12:1).

The Luminous Mysteries

The Baptism of Jesus. "And when Jesus had been baptized, just as he came up from the water, suddenly the heavens were opened to him and he saw the Spirit of God descending like a dove and alighting on him" (Matthew 3:16).

The Wedding Feast of Cana. "When the wine gave out, the mother of Jesus said to him, 'They have no wine.' … His mother said to the servants, 'Do whatever he tells you'" (John 2:3,5).

Proclamation of the Kingdom. "From that time Jesus began to proclaim, 'Repent, for the kingdom of heaven has come near'" (Matthew 4:17).

The Transfiguration. "And while he was praying, the appearance of his face changed, and his clothes became dazzling white….Then, from a cloud came a voice that said, 'This is my Son, my Chosen; listen to him!'" (Luke 9:29,35).

Institution of the Eucharist. "While they were eating, he took a loaf of bread, and after blessing it he broke it, gave it to them, and said, 'Take; this is my body' (Mark 14:22).

HOW We Live It

- *How can the various prayer forms help you grow in your faith and spiritual practice?*

- *What other prayers are important to you? Research other Catholic prayers that will help increase your prayer vocabulary.*

Conclude the session by praying the Lord's Prayer:

Our Father, who art in heaven,
hallowed be thy name;
thy kingdom come, thy will be done
on earth as it is in heaven.
Give us this day our daily bread;
and forgive us our trespasses;
as we forgive those who trespass against us;
and lead us not into temptation,
but deliver us from evil. Amen.

SUGGESTED RESOURCES

Campbell-Johnston, Michael. *In the Midst of Noise: An Ignatian Retreat in Everyday Life.*

Papandrea, James L. *Pray (Not Just Say) the Lord's Prayer.*

Powell, Philip Neri. *Treasures Old and New: Traditional Prayers for Today's Catholics.*

Wright, Wendy M. *The Essential Spirituality Handbook.*

Concluding Prayer: O God, we thank you for the gift of Church. Help us see ourselves as valuable members of the body of Christ, each with unique gifts and talents that we bring to the community of faith. Open our eyes to the beauty of your work in all people and in all places, and grant us the grace to grow in faith and love. Amen.